DATING:
THE VIRGIN
GUIDE

D1549160

Also published by Virgin Books:

Buying a Home: The Virgin Guide
Entertaining: The Virgin Guide
Money: The Virgin Guide

DATING: THE VIRGIN GUIDE

Nicole Carmichael

BOOKS

First published in Great Britain in 2003 by
Virgin Books Ltd
Thames Wharf Studios
Rainville Road
London
W6 9HA

All the information contained in this book, including addresses, telephone numbers
and prices, was correct at the time of going to press. However, such information
is subject to change.

ISBN 0 7535 0741 2

Typeset by Phoenix Photosetting, Chatham, Kent
Printed and bound in Great Britain by Mackays of Chatham

CONTENTS

INTRODUCTION

Boyfriends? No thanks. I'd rather stay at home with a copy of the Radio Times and a highlighter pen.
(my great friend) Julie Adams, circa 2000

Everyone around you seems to be having a better time than you are. You're sick of being desperate and dateless on a Saturday night, going on holiday with fellow singletons and cursing Bridget Jones for making your life a cliché. You may have had several failed relationships in the past, or maybe it's your 'unique' small talk that scares potential dates away? The bottom line is you're single and you're not happy about it. Maybe you think that dating is just about luck and nothing else? If that's the case then this practical guide is just for you. It not only offers dating and relationship advice, from where to track down potential romance to how to deal with ex-girlfriend/boyfriend syndrome. It also analyses why you feel you need to find Mr/Ms Right at this time of your life, and establishes what you should be looking for in a partner.

Even if you think that you are a loser magnet, this book will help you spot similar patterns in your own relationships so that you can avoid making the same mistakes again. The guide also shows you how to boost your confidence, widen your social circles and learn from positive and negative dating experiences. It explores dating agencies, lonely hearts and Internet dating, plus some more unconventional ways of making a match, including text flirting, astral love, speed dating and date coaching. It also explains the nuts and bolts of body language and flirting skills to help you make the most of any potential dating opportunity. You could soon be out there meeting Mr/Ms Nice and making sweet music together – or at least giving yourself more of a chance to.

I don't promise to have you married off by page 200 (if I could do that I would have made a lot more money by now) but hopefully you'll soon be enjoying yourself more, whether you're going out and trying new things or just laughing about other people's dating disasters.

By the way, all of the case studies are totally true – hand on heart – but I've kept them (mostly) anonymous to save embarrassment (partly my own as some of the stories happened to me!). The case studies tend to fall into a similar age group – from 26–40, but that doesn't mean that if you're younger or older then the information isn't relevant for you. And although some of the information may seem quite obvious, it's amazing how many people make the same mistakes over and over again, so just think of it as a bit of practical revision!

Having scratched the surface of the 'singles world', I've uncovered a whole dating culture out there with plenty of opportunities for making great friends and possibly even meeting your life partner. There's really no excuse for being single if you don't want to be. As numerous dating experts have told me throughout the course of writing this book, it's a numbers game and the more people you meet and the more positive steps you take to get yourself out of the singles rut, the more effective your love life will be. So what are you waiting for?

Happy dating,

Nicole

1 WHAT'S STOPPING YOU?

What's stopping you dating and why is it so scary? The preconceived notions of dating, versus what happens in real life to real people like you.

Since the 90s the single scene has just exploded in the UK. In the 2000 National Census there were four million unattached 25–44 year olds and according to a Government survey carried out at the time, nearly 50 per cent of older singles say they are happier than they were five years ago. It's a brave new world for single people out there and far from having the 'desperate and dateless' stigma attached to them, dating agencies and singles' societies are seriously fashionable. Suddenly it's hip to be single – and very hip to try the dating game. Instead of all being sad Bridget Jones types we can all celebrate the *Sex and the City* culture and get out there and have some serious fun.

People don't want to tie themselves down when there's so much fun to be had out there. Single people want to do more shopping around before settling down. That's why the idea of 'dating' rather than 'going out with someone' has become much more popular recently. American TV shows and modern movies focus on the idea of having several dates with various people rather than one monogamous relationship. Variety, it seems, is definitely the spice of life and it's a liberating idea that you can meet someone, be mutually attracted to them and casually arrange a date – without making any grand statements or promises that you are now an 'item'. You go out, you have fun and decide whether you're going to see them again. End of story. Meanwhile, you could be seeing several other people at the same time who have the same agenda as you, no heavy relationships, promises or soul searching as to whether you have found Mr/Ms Right. All that can come later, much further down the line. Dating is just about going out on dates, meeting up with someone for an hour, an evening or just a cup of coffee, the 'date' idea simply being that there's an undercurrent of romance potential between the two of you.

It's hard for us Brits to get our heads around the concept of dating more than one person at one time, especially as we have had it drummed into us from an early age that two-timing is such a no-no. You go out with one person, if it doesn't work out, you break up and then the next one comes along and so on. The conflict of dating versus two timing depends of course on how far you want to take your date – whether you are saying 'let's meet up again' at the end of the evening or the following morning when you wake up together. But that's an entirely personal issue. One thing this book isn't going to tell you is when you should sleep with someone for the first time (and I'm not talking about catching forty winks). It's completely up to you whether you sleep with someone on the first date or wait until you have both said your vows at the altar (or wherever). The important thing is to do what feels right for you and never be pressured into doing anything unless you feel totally happy with the situation.

When it comes to the rules of dating, you can take advice from the experts but you should always listen to your own instincts about how you would like to play a relationship. The premise of Ellen Fein and Sherrie Schneider's best selling American dating book *The Rules* is that 'Man pursues Woman' and not the other way around. There are many other rules for various scenarios, including 'Be a creature unlike any other', all of which, Ellen and Sherrie declare, boast phenomenal success rates and could certainly work for you. The point is that it's up to you to decide whether you want to try out 'dating' – that idea that you can go out with strings of different people, doing a bit of a pick and mix to decide which direction you'd like your love life to head in next – or if you'd prefer just to carry on the way that you've always done things with consecutive relationships.

The crux of the matter is, whether you just want to go out for the occasional date or be part of a full-blown relationship, if you're not getting past the daydreaming, wishing and hoping stage then there must be something standing in your way. We all have friends who we think are lovely looking, have great personalities and seem to have everything going for them. We can't understand why they're still single and neither, they say, can they. If we're so successful at making friends and making the rest of our lives happen the way we want them to, why the glitch with dating? You may be one such person.

It could be that your past relationships and dating experiences have been such unmitigated disasters that the idea of trying again literally brings you out in a cold sweat. You could have been very hurt in the past and simply can't face going through the same kind of heartache again. Or it could be that the preconceived notions of dating seem so remote from your own circumstances that there's a distinct lack of realistic role models and situations for you to learn anything useful from.

It's hardly surprising that people get hung up about the 'rules' of dating and relationships when we're constantly bombarded with movies, TV shows, love songs and romantic fiction that follow a framework of scenarios. Take the classic chick flick or trashy romantic paperback novel for example: single girl meets man (through whichever quirky circumstance the writer decides to plot), they fall in love, probably fall out along the way, but ultimately fall into each other's arms. Simplistic maybe, but the fact is that the majority of fictional plots follow these predictable highs and lows. Of course it's not all happy ever after – there are plenty of love stories that leave you sobbing into your Kleenex and adamant that you'll never love again, just in case you have to go through the kind of torment that the cinematic sweethearts have just endured. Heart-breaking death scenes and fairy-tale weddings have got a lot to answer for.

What's more, celebrities seem to have their own set of rules when it comes to relationships. They too seem to love the fairy-tale romances and the big flashy weddings (for the media opportunities if nothing else) but they don't seem to be able to handle the dull real-life stuff and suddenly the relationship is over almost as quickly as it started. It's almost as if they too believe in the roles that they play.

Then of course there's the mundane drudgery of coupledom in soap operas and TV dramas, leading us to believe that all relationships are so uninspiring that even the most devoted duos will contemplate affairs at one time or another – usually with someone who lives in the same street!

Of course there are more realistic examples, but quirkier storylines tend to make better TV and a novel about 'normal' life where nothing especially remarkable happens isn't going to top any bestsellers or ratings. If you need any more convincing that fiction is a million miles away from what happens in the real world watch *Sex and the City*. The fact that four beautiful, successful and sussed females in New York can't find an equally sorted mate among them doesn't bode well for the rest of us lesser lip-glossed mere mortals. Similarly, when the world's most handsome men get cast as tragic bachelors in major Hollywood movies one can't help feeling cynical.

If you're single (and you don't want to be) your first step is to take all those fictional love stories with a huge pinch of salt. Remember, those love stories that we see on screen are just entertainment for entertainment's sake and are seldom based on any kind of fact. Once you start realising that knights in shining armour and beautiful damsels in distress are literally the stuff of fairy stories then you're on the right track. If you start basing relationships on fictional role models then you're heading for a fall.

Now all you have to do is get to grips with everyone else's preconceived notions of romance – and find out what *you* really want. This is easier said than done of course when everyone around you believes they are some kind of part-time Cupid and 'have this really great friend who you'll just love'. Then you end up going on yet another disastrous blind date and wondering why on earth you ever agreed to it – and how on earth your 'so-called' friend could have believed you two would hit it off together. A friend of mine went on a blind date with someone and couldn't believe the troll who turned up to meet her. He was super intelligent which was definitely on my friend's checklist of requirements, but he started picking his teeth almost as soon as the food arrived, tutted heavily when he heard she was a journalist and contradicted everything that she said. At one point my friend thought Jeremy Beadle would appear with a camera because the whole thing had to be a joke, but afterwards her friend who had set it up was really surprised that they hadn't hit it off. Another friend went on a disastrous blind date with someone who she had been fixed up with and when she asked her personal Cupid about it later she was told,

'Oh, I felt sorry for him because he hasn't dated for years and I thought you'd be a good listener for him.' So much for sexual solidarity.

It can often seem that everyone from your parents to your closest friends intrinsically believes that everyone else wants to be in a couple, choosing to forget that the word 'bachelor' and 'spinster' only exist if they're prefixed by the word 'lonely'. Bridget Jones coined a phrase when she called couples 'smug marrieds' and every single person on the planet must have experienced those cringe-inducing scenarios when 'smug marrieds' quiz you about your love life, with a liberal dose of 'never mind, you'll meet the right person one day' sentiments. It's almost as if being single is some kind of embarrassing disease that they'd really rather not be privy to.

And when they're not trying to be matchmakers or worldly wise philosophers they'll bulldoze you with 'you never know, it could happen to you' heart-warming stories. Tales of a friend of a friend who was adamant that she'd never meet Mr Right, then she got together with someone she'd known for years but didn't think she fancied and they now have three wonderful children, blah blah blah.

Granted, those scenarios do happen and there are lots of case studies in this book to prove that love really can happen in the strangest circumstances. But if you can be more proactive about dating and forming relationships rather than letting everyone else make all the decisions for you, you are much more likely to get results. It's true, you may eventually meet your soulmate through one of your best friends, but relying on being fixed up by someone who has known you all your life may not be the best course for you. It's time to start thinking for yourself and looking deeper.

But before you go any further and start planning how to go about meeting more potential dates, you have to decide whether you really want a relationship or have just been bamboozled by all those matchmakers around you. Dating and being part of a relationship can be fun but there are no guarantees that it's for everyone. Some people will be happier on their own, no matter what happens. For every happy-ever-after story there are a dozen false starts.

Remember, you have to kiss an awful lot of frogs before you find your prince (or princess). You will ultimately be able to learn from dating mistakes (especially the ones that are really embarrassing) and you'll be able just to move on. But if you let yourself get hurt over and over again it can't help but chip away further at your self-esteem. When push comes to shove and you start evaluating the circumstances of where your life is going at the moment you may find that there simply isn't room for anyone else in your life, emotionally or physically. And that's absolutely fine. You may find that you have been taking your own space for granted and what with your social life, current hobbies, work and other commitments you're actually pretty happy thank you very much. You can just carry on with your fantastic life and you can answer that nagging question of 'Why are you still single?' with 'Because I want to be.'

If you are still coming up with the same conclusions – that you don't want to be single but you don't know how to go about dating successfully, then this book's for you. Whether you want to try the *Sex and the City* approach and go out for lots of dates with several people on a casual basis, or meet Mr/Ms Right and fall hopelessly in love, this book will guide you in the right directions. From where to find drop-dead gorgeous, available, single people like yourself to how to flirt with them successfully, carry off that crucial first date and maybe even sail into the sunset together.

Be prepared though, you may need to change your ideas about dating and you'll almost certainly have to take some risks. Let's face it, the love of your life isn't just going to appear in your living room one night while you're sitting at home watching telly and biting your fingernails. (OK, it may do if your flatmate happens to know a legion of eligible fellow singletons, but let's be realistic here.) The bottom line is you'll have to make some kind of effort to learn the dating game and the first thing you need to learn about is yourself.

PICTURE THIS

Think about the way others may see you. Look closely at recent photos of yourself and see if you can remember how you were feeling at the precise time that the photo was taken.

Ask yourself:

→ **How did you feel about the person taking the photograph?**
→ **Did you like them?**
→ **Does the expression on your face match up with how you were feeling at the time?**
→ **Do you try and hide your feelings?**
→ **Do you smile naturally and easily or find that you often cover up your mouth with your hand?**
→ **Do you look wary of people in photographs?**

Similarly, look at any video recordings there may be of you and notice how you interact with people and how you react to what they say. Can you hide your disdain for someone you don't like? And do you go all misty-eyed if you're with someone you fancy? Sometimes our friends can see us flirting before we even know we're doing it – faces are incredibly expressive, but can also be misleading. Confidence can be construed as arrogance, shyness can be read as detachment, friendliness can be seen as overt flirting and so on. Try and get to grips with the characteristics of your own body language and analyse your own particular mannerisms. You don't have to turn yourself into an amateur anthropologist, but it's easy subconsciously to give off misleading information. It's also easy to learn how to correct mannerisms, which may not be doing you any favours. You can't change habits overnight, but you can quickly learn things about yourself, which may have been standing in your way for years.

FACE FACTS

Ask your closest friend how they think you come over to other people. Tell him/her to be honest otherwise there's no point in the exercise.

→ **Maybe you are so self-assertive that the people you are attracted to are intimidated by you and believe that you are so confident and single-minded that you wouldn't think twice about having anything to do with them.**
→ **Maybe the combination of you and your friends on a usual night out gives off the wrong signals. A group of fabulous-looking girls laughing and joking together in a nightclub may not actually be doing themselves any favours at all in the romance stakes.**
→ **You may think you're the most fun person in the world to be with: you're witty, friendly and know how to have a good time, but others may see**

you as loud, threatening, silly and a bit of a handful. Be careful about collective body language as well as your own. (See Chapter 4 for more details.)

SO NATURAL

Basic attraction comes through eye contact. The size of the pupils, the length of the shared glance and the accompanying expression can all add up to sexual attraction and if it's done with the correct thought process behind it you're going to get even more results. Without having to dress up, make any particular effort or any grand leap of faith into the world of dating, a look can speak volumes. And it stands to reason that a warm, open, natural smile is more appealing than a scowl. It's the whole basis of good customer service after all. So break into a smile more often and see the reaction you get.

Stop looking around you for the right person and be that person yourself. You may be looking for someone warm, kind, sincere and amusing, but it's likely that every other single person will be too. Let's face it, they're unlikely to be looking for someone who's cold, mean, insincere and with no sense of humour. Instead of making a checklist of all of the qualities that you are looking for, make sure that you fit your own criteria. If you'd like to date someone that is easy-going and friendly, then you have to give off similar vibes, even if you don't naturally feel relaxed about doing so. You may often be attracted to people with a good sense of humour, but if you stand around with a face like thunder and appear totally unapproachable then you are more likely to scare someone off. Of course, it's human nature to be shy and you may be painfully so, but you may have to adapt some things about your personality and your mannerisms in order to make things happen.

LEARN FROM OTHERS

Start evaluating occasions where there's potential for finding a date and look at how other people behave.

→ People-watching is a great way to pick up dating techniques, but be subtle about it – you don't want to be accused of stalking or of being a nosy parker! See how strangers interact with each other in bars and other public places. Look at their eye contact, expressions and other mannerisms.

→ In a one-to-one situation, any form of crossed arms or legs is supposedly a way of holding oneself back and being closed off, as is avoiding eye contact. If someone is being obviously chatted up, see how quickly the 'chatter up' gets the message if there is no eye contact and more obviously, if the person they are working on starts looking elsewhere in the room.

→ Look at any couple that is using their hands to stress a point. People that communicate in a more animated way immediately attract more attention, but see how effective their moves are. Are they endearing themselves to the other person? Or do they just come over as a little eccentric?

Before you start your own dating communication campaign, check out the success (or otherwise) of other people's moves and give yourself a head start.

KNOW YOURSELF, BUT DON'T BE A KNOW-ALL

As well as paying close attention to your body language, reassess the way you voice your opinions. It's one thing being able to hold a conversation, quite another to bully others with your views, or patronise them about theirs. Just as confident mannerisms can appear intimidating, so can clear-cut opinions and unbending ideals. Never let it be suggested that a female shouldn't be single-minded, but faced with a very strong-willed opinionated female, the less confident male (bless him) is even less likely to make the first move. If you're playing the dating game, the fewer hurdles you both have to get over, the better the end results are likely to be. Listen to yourself more and when you think you're winding yourself up into a confrontation or becoming extra determined to prove a point, back off a little. Take stock of the situation and how your reactions may be adversely affecting what started out as a simple conversation.

Getting the most out of relationships starts with showing yourself to your best advantage. We all have off days, but that total stranger who you'd like to get to know doesn't need to see the fact that you have a really bad temper and possibly some rather embarrassing hang-ups about the opposite sex. We'll discuss chatting-up etiquette later on in the book, but it should go without saying that you really don't need to tell anyone the history of your love life within minutes – or days for that matter – of meeting them. One of the keys to a successful relationship (and there are so, so many) is to take everything very slowly and make the right decisions for yourself.

The thing that's ultimately stopping you dating is you. Either your dating techniques aren't doing you any favours and are a little rusty/peculiar/non-existent, or those preconceived notions of dating are holding you back. It could also be that your 'so-called' friends are taking the decision-making out of your hands, introducing you to a sad bunch of singletons that make you feel even worse about yourself. Or they keep trying to pair you off with people who have nothing in common with you other than the same number of limbs. If that's the case then maybe you should consider editing your friends if necessary. Try and surround yourself with people who make you feel good and bring out the best in you, rather than ones who compound your personal doubts and fears.

Start getting more proactive. Think about what you want in life and set about getting it. It's very easy to let one weekend drift into another, making arrangements to do things with friends that are 'safe' – dinner at each other's houses, going to the cinema or the local pub. But if those environments haven't worked for you before romantically, then it's time to start doing things differently and making the most of any potential date-creating opportunities. Chapter 6 explores ways to widen your social circles and basically get out more to places where you are likely to meet more single people, without having to appear desperate and dateless at the same time. You'll open up your social horizons and meet new friends who in turn will know more single people, and so on.

One of the best and most useful sayings which is also a self-help book is *Feel the Fear and Do It Anyway*, written by Susan Jeffers (published by Rider)*. This is the concept that nothing can actually be as scary as the idea of the thing itself. Therefore if you truly

*See Further Reading

believe that dating is terrifying, any kind of situation cannot possibly live up to how bad you think it could be. In any case, if you do the dating thing properly it can be masses of fun – it must be, otherwise nobody would do it in the first place! True, you might make a bit of a twit of yourself along the way, but one thing's for sure, you'll learn a lot about the type of person you truly are. And how can that be bad?

CASE STUDY

37-year-old Jenny, a singing teacher from London, is typical of many thirty-something women. She has had a couple of serious relationships, several short-term love affairs and plenty of dating disappointments...

I think that the main problem about dating as you get older is supply and demand. In my twenties I met single people all the time but in your thirties you don't meet that many single men. I also think you get used to be being on your own. You can quite happily tell yourself that you're happy being single and convince yourself and others that you're fine about it, but I think that everybody wants to be with somebody really, even if they don't admit it. For example, it would be nice on a Sunday night to have someone to sit with, eat with and watch a bit of TV with. I know it's a cliché but if you are looking at a beautiful scene it's better sharing it with someone, and if you're having a bad day it's better to be able to share your problems with someone as well. I'm not trying to pretend that relationships are easy, but it's nice to have a person there to share things with – the fact that no matter how trivial the subject may be, you can still tell someone about it.

I don't think that I am actually at the stage where I am so desperate that I'm really going to act differently to make things happen for me. It's one thing saying it and it's another doing it! I've been on a lot of dates with people in the last few years and I have asked people out, so it's not as if I'm not proactive, but I always meet people through friends, at parties and through work. I'd never just walk up to a stranger and start talking to them.

I think it's easy to get into the habit of seeing a lot of the same people. You can have a nice time and meet up with your friends on Saturday and go round to someone's house for Sunday lunch but it's very rare to meet new men – unless you work with them. It's like walking up the high street every day, never going into a clothes shop and still expecting to find a new frock – it's not going to happen.

I think there's a big difference between making an effort to find a boyfriend and being absolutely desperate to have one and I think it's quite hard to strike that balance. I think everyone has that ideal that they are just going to meet someone and that it's contrived to meet people in unusual ways like dating agencies. If you meet someone through your friends you immediately feel you have something in common already – you know that they are probably nice people because they are friends of your friends and it's quite a good filtering process. But when you meet people through the Internet or another 'contrived' way it's a leap into the unknown.

I've been on a couple of blind dates and I've got there and I've thought, 'I don't fancy you, there's absolutely no chemistry and oh God, I've got to spend an entire evening with you,' and I've actually found it quite painful. There's something depressing about the idea of turning up at a blind date and either not fancying them or seeing the immediate expression on their face that they don't fancy you. Whether you go on dinner dates or try lonely hearts you are still exposing yourself and basically saying, 'I want a relationship, are you going to be that person?' You can go for the friendship thing, but I've got this romantic idea in my head about meeting the right person 'naturally', but then my rational mind tells me that's ridiculous and that if it was going to happen it would have already happened by now.

Dating can give you amazing highs but also amazing lows and I think single people fall into two categories: they are either depressed about being single, in which case they won't make the effort to change anything, or they're not worried enough about being single. Either way I think that they will find it difficult to meet people. The depressed ones will give off desperate vibes and the ones that say they are happy about it won't really make enough effort to meet people. I suppose it's all about striking a balance really. Hopefully this book will tell me how to do that. . .

CASE STUDY

35-year-old Susan has different views on being single:

I've been single in my life more often than I've been in a couple, but I don't actually see being single as a label in the same way that I don't label my friends who are married or mothers and so on. I see people as people. I think if you are determined to see yourself as 'single' then it dominates your life and everything becomes shaded by the fact that you haven't got a boyfriend.

People don't tend to believe me when I say that I'm quite happy the way that I am and assume that most single people lie around all the time crying and feeling crap about themselves. But even when you go out with people you feel like that sometimes – you can still feel lonely even if you're with someone. When you're crying about not having a boyfriend, it rarely has anything to do with the fact you're single, you're crying because you're miserable and you want someone to make you feel better. So you pick on the thing that would make you feel better, rather than the thing that's really the cause of the misery.

I went through this period once where I thought, 'Right, I'm going start dating,' because all I do is sit at home. And unless I'm going to go out with the gas man I don't think I'm ever going to meet someone! So for a whole year I told everyone that I was looking to go on dates and did about fifteen or twenty blind dates in a year and it taught me some very valuable things. Number one, that there are lots of really appropriate men out there – so when women say there are no single men it's just crap, because there are. Number two, that prior to going on these dates I thought if I could meet a nice man that was perhaps 40 per cent of what I wanted (rather than 70 or 80) then I'd be quite happy to make a go of it because I felt really lonely at the time. But what I realised after going on these dates is you can't do that because it's not fair to them and it's not fair to you. And that it's better to be on your own than with someone who doesn't make you feel happy.

I came to realise that, OK I haven't got a boyfriend, but I'm really happy. I've got really wonderful friends, a wonderful family, a really fulfilling career and a life that I can do what I want with, so to feel sad because I haven't got a boyfriend somehow negates the plusses. I hate saying this because I think it makes me sound arrogant but I genuinely don't know why I don't have a boyfriend. I think at the end of the day it's more circumstance than a huge flaw in my personality because everything else is so right. Therefore I can't feel sad about it; I just think there'll be people out there and the right situation and the right time, but it doesn't mean everything to me at the moment.

I'm not saying that I never want to meet anyone, because I do. I want to share my life with someone and I feel I have a lot to share, but I feel that's in the future, not now. When you're single you can sometimes see your life stretching onwards the same way and it is depressing and you think there may come a time when you're the only single person on earth. When you get older you can feel more alone, especially if you don't make an effort to build a community around you with your friends and family, but I make a point of doing that.

My friend's mum says, 'You never know your luck at a picnic,' and I think it's so true. You never know where you are going to meet someone. I've met people in all sorts of places – I met someone on the bus and another guy who served me a cup of coffee in a café, a couple of guys at parties and a guy through work. If you start thinking that you aren't going to meet anybody and there's no one out there then the chances are that you won't see the opportunity because you close yourself off to it. Someone will talk to you on the bus and you'll think they're a nutter, or you'll decide that you're not going to let the person who's serving you coffee chat you up because he's not on the same career ladder as you are. It's like having a really strict shopping list of requirements for a boyfriend and it makes you really judgemental about people.

You have to have an idea of what you are looking for but be flexible about it. On the one hand I want a man who will really look after me, but on the other hand I want a really independent man who doesn't cramp my life, so those two things contradict each other and they're not realistic. I think it's really good to go on dates, even if someone asks you out and it's not really right, because it's really good for your confidence, it's fun and I think you should see every date as a learning experience.

DATING DATA – POINTS TO REMEMBER
WHAT'S STOPPING YOU?

→ Think about what is really stopping you from dating. Is it the preconceived notions of dating or your own real-life experiences? (More about your past in Chapter 2!)

→ Start being more proactive about dating and don't allow others to play Cupid all of the time.

→ Evaluate your life to decide why you want / need another person in your life.

→ Realise that you might have to take some risks and be prepared to learn some home truths.

→ Ask friends for constructive opinions about how you come across to them.

→ Be aware of your own body language – and other people's. Start 'people-watching' more.

→ Work on showing your best side.

→ Think about what you want out of a relationship and set about getting it.

2 LEARNING LESSONS FROM THE PAST

*How to analyse your past experiences and learn from them –
without the aid of a highly paid therapist!*

The reason dating seems to get more difficult as we get older has a
great deal to do with the emotional baggage that increases as we
tackle various relationships. We start off as teenagers with a clean
slate but bad experiences colour our viewpoints and it's very much
a case of once bitten, twice shy – multiplied by however many
relationships there have been that have fallen by the wayside. That
first love can have a lot to answer for. You might have had a major
infatuation at thirteen years old and still feel a little bruised
emotionally – twenty years on.

Anyone who has had a broken heart is naturally reluctant to fall in
love again because as you notch up more failed romances, so your
own emotional baggage increases. You get to a point where you
think all men are bastards, or all women are bitches, and you just
don't want to tempt fate with another relationship, just in case you
get hurt again. It's only natural. But you can use past experiences
to your advantage in order to understand why certain relationships
would never have worked in the first place and as a barometer for
future dating experiences.

It's completely normal for your trust to be undermined when a
relationship has failed, and it's common to tar everyone with the
same brush. The difficulty is to get your head around the fact that
everyone is different. Once you start to look at a person as an
individual, as opposed to one of a race of 'global bastards', then you
can start actually to work out what went wrong before. You have to
start breaking down the situation and ask yourself what part you
played in its downfall, so that you can be wary about the way you
act or react in the future. Then, if you ever find yourself in a similar
position, you can recognise the warning signs and rectify the
situation accordingly.

'When we're hurting, the first thing that we do is look around for someone to blame and focus our anger on in order to start to move forward. It's a natural form of self-preservation,' says Denise Knowles, spokesperson for Relate relationship counselling. 'In partner relationships we blame the other person for whatever went wrong and then if we find ourselves in the same situation again we say, "It's nothing to do with me – all men are bastards," and so the cycle continues.'

TAKING THE LEAD

You have to do away with the context of blame and look at your part in the relationship. If you feel that this relationship is going down the same road as the one before and the one before that, at that point you have to stop and take stock of what you are doing. It's not about turning the blame on yourself, it's just recognising at which point something started to go wrong and making a conscious decision to try and handle the situation differently.

For example, if you feel yourself being taken for granted and the relationship appears strangely familiar, think 'Hang on a minute, I've been here before.' If he/she expects you to be available whenever he/she picks up the telephone, say 'I'm sorry, I can't make it – give me a bit more notice.' You may not have anything else to do at all and you might be kicking yourself because you want to see him/her *so much*, but sometimes you've got to play harder to get – and it really works. When a friend of mine 'suddenly' developed a whole social life that her boyfriend wasn't involved in, she was suddenly hot property. She told him that she could only see him on certain days of the week and it was incredible how compliant he suddenly became. Take control and you'll be making it clear that you're not going to be there just to be picked up and put down. If you find yourself thinking, 'Here I go again', stop and turn the situation to your own advantage. Before you go down the road of being very hurt again, you can nip it in the bud, recognise the problem and act differently on it. This should help you to stop thinking that you attract the wrong type of person, or that you are simply no good at handling relationships. You can be good at handling relationships, you just need to work on the early stages and create a springboard for the rest of the relationship.

MAPPING THE FUTURE

Another positive thing to come out of a bad relationship is knowing what you don't want in the future. It's a foundation for how you can build a good relationship the next time. Denise Knowles says, 'Draw yourself a line and map all the good things that happened in the relationship above the line. The things that start falling below the line are the negatives and if those incidents happen again, you should say to yourself, "No, I've been there, I didn't like it and I'm not going there again." You can use those negative experiences to your own advantage, highlight where you don't want to be again and use that as a framework for the future.'

REMEMBER WHO YOU ARE

People often say that they feel they've lost sight of who they are in a relationship and that's because you've attempted to be the person you believe he/she wants you to be. If you are going into a relationship you have to be yourself. If you're not a demure person, don't attempt to be. You'll only look daft when you fall over in your slingbacks or you meet up with a gang of your mates and they laugh at your pseudo sophisticated-lady impersonation. Obviously you may have to temper your behaviour for certain situations – basic good manners are useful if you don't want to scare someone off! A friend of mine likes nothing more than a really good belch after she finishes a meal and actually gets quite defensive if anyone says 'Ugh!' Then she wonders why she's still single. . .

With every situation you'll need to test the water a little. If you get to the 'meet the parents' stage then you might have to keep your personality in check a little if it's, let's say, a little larger than life, but for goodness sake don't try and be someone you're not. It's certain that you will be found out eventually and it could be the downfall of the relationship.

TAKE IT SLOWLY

The next time you find yourself in a relationship don't be sucked in by fantastic words, gestures, text messages and amazing promises that happen very early on in the relationship. What you should be aiming for is to have a friendship with someone, whether you are just dating or wanting to form 'the' relationship of your life. Friendships develop over a much longer period of time and you need to get to know someone warts and all.

If you start getting heavy duty declarations of love very early on, enjoy it, but also be cautious – particularly if you have a bad dating track record which will tend to make you even more vulnerable. So the first time someone shows you that type of affection, don't allow yourself to be lulled into a false sense of security. You don't need to be cynical either, but be cautious and do a reality check every now and again and keep control. Keep on top of the expectations that you both have for the relationship.

'The dating world is like sitting on a fast train and seeing the countryside flashing by in snapshots through the window,' says Denise Knowles. 'With relationships we are living so fast that we are getting a brief snapshot of everything that we see and we feel and we don't spend the time exploring and understanding what it is that's really going on. All we recognise is the end result. If anything starts to go wrong we think, this isn't working and last time I ended up getting hurt so I'm not doing it again. Whereas the thing to do is to slow down and believe that if anything is worthwhile it's worth spending time on it.'

If you really like chocolate, think about how much more you enjoy it when you sit down and eat it really slowly and savour every chunk, rather than gobbling it down and hardly letting it touch the side of your mouth. If something is going to be a pleasurable experience, enjoy it and take it slowly.

PICTURE THE FUTURE

Pete Cohen, life strategist and author of *Habit Busting* and *Fear Busting* says that the way forward in any situation is to make a picture in your mind of the life that you want. 'A baby doesn't see things going wrong, it sees what it wants,' he says. 'He sees someone walking and chooses to do the same thing, even though it's not easy. He won't just start walking – it's a process of falling over and just doing it again, but he'll learn how not to make the same mistakes again.' Unfortunately people just carry on making the same bad decisions with dating again and again. 'It's like the Englishman in Paris who says "Where's the Eiffel tower?" and when he doesn't get a response he just says it louder and louder and can't see why he isn't getting an answer,' says Pete Cohen. 'If you don't recognise what you are doing wrong in any situation and if you can't put the past behind you and move on, you'll just keep being haunted by things that went wrong and similar scenarios will happen again and again.'

DON'T PICTURE THE PAST

'People say, "I hope that experience doesn't happen to me again,"' continues Pete Cohen, 'but the very nature of saying something like that is putting a picture of something negative into your head. It's like me saying to you, "Don't think of cheese!" What's the first thing that comes into your head? Exactly, cheese! The thing to do is to make positive, not negative pictures of what you want for your own future.'

The theory of self-fulfilment suggests that if you picture something happening it will. On a recent trip abroad I was drinking black coffee and wearing a pair of white trousers and just as I was thinking wouldn't it be awful to spill the coffee all over them I did just that. Similarly, if a woman truly thinks that all men are bastards then when she meets a man, one way or another she'll turn into the victim again. Many people who have been physically abused in a relationship find themselves with someone who is identical to their ex. It's so common, Pete Cohen says, because people get 'comfortable' with a certain situation, be it a good or bad experience. 'They learn to develop a mental comfort zone with self-talk. They have invested so much into their own comfort zone that if they had a pound for every time they talked or acted a certain way, they'd be millionaires!'

To change any situation you have to do things differently, and you have to focus on a different way of thinking and the result that you would like to see. As far as dating is concerned, how bad would it be if you focused on just enjoying yourself rather than picturing the rest of your life together? Just having fun with someone who wants to have a good time themselves. Go on, be a devil, go on a few blind dates. OK, they might seem scary, but just think of them more as a light-hearted social experiment than some heavy agenda for the rest of your life. If the date doesn't work out, what's the worst thing that can happen? As long as you follow the dating dos and don'ts (see Chapter 10) you can just put it down to experience and move on.

REBOUND DATING

That said, it's incredibly difficult not to be affected by past relationships and the timing has to be right before you start embarking on the dating scene again after a relationship hasn't worked out. Going out with people on the rebound won't do either of you any favours. Even if you try and convince yourself that you're only doing it for a bit of fun, your feelings will come to the surface a little later, that's all. And no one is likely to want to spend serious time with you if you are bitter, twisted and hard-hearted, so spend time getting over past relationships and take time out from trying to find the right person to remember who you are yourself. If you aren't yourself, then how are you going to find the person who will be right for you? You're just more likely to clock up more dating disasters. You should look on dating as a chance to have some fun and meet new people, but you have to be in the right mindset from the word go. Keep telling yourself that every person is an individual and no two relationships will ever be the same; it's up to you to create a clean slate for the new relationship to have the best possible start.

Of course it isn't easy to forget totally the past and try and emerge as a butterfly rather than a bedraggled jittery moth after a relationship has failed. Even if we are aware of our failings it doesn't mean that we can instantly make ourselves a better person. Habits are hard to break. Just keep in mind that people often end up treating you in the way that you expect to be treated. It's a self-fulfilling prophecy. You may act or react to certain situations in a way that causes other people to act in a certain way. For example, if you put on a babyish voice, you are going to be treated like less of an adult than you really are. Shows like *Big Brother* prove that when you take on subservient roles, people quickly grow more dominant. In the same way, psychologists say in order to stop your self-fulfilling prophecy that you are always treated badly, you should allow the other person to be who they are and not try and direct their actions by your own insecurities.

CASE STUDY

31-year-old Cathy, a dental nurse from south London, has done some serious thinking after she realised her relationships were becoming strangely familiar.

I've just come out of a relationship that seemed to be on fast forward from the word go. I was bowled over by a man called Greg who knew that I've had crappy relationships in the past and said that he'd make up for all of the love that I'd been missing out on. He took me away to fantastic hotels for weekends; he bought me clothes, fantastic meals and convinced me that our relationship was the best thing since sliced bread. On the days when we weren't together, Greg sent me sweet text messages and always called me when he said he would. He even said things like 'You're stuck with me now for ever,' and I just lapped it up. I didn't put him under any pressure to make any kind of commitment to me, but one day he just turned cold on me. He said he just realised I wasn't 'the one' and suddenly didn't feel the same way any more about me. He wouldn't talk it through or try and work out what had happened, it was just over as quickly as it had begun.

Looking back, it was exactly the pattern of the relationship that I'd had with Adam, the guy I went out with before Greg. I was totally full-on with him – he sent me romantic love letters, bought me presents and very quickly moved in with me. It was all incredibly fast. A few months into the relationship I went on holiday with a friend and when I came home he had taken all his stuff and moved out, just like that. He also said that his feelings had suddenly changed and he didn't know why.

I've done some long, hard thinking and I know that if you get into that kind of fast-track relationship, it can't survive. It's just not real. If I'd taken control and put the brakes on, both relationships could have stood more of a chance. It wouldn't have been so heavy from the word go. Those first few months in a relationship are crucial and you can both get totally absorbed and infatuated, but those kinds of relationships can never last. At least, I know they can't for me. I've got over the 'all men are bastards' stage now and understand that I have to tread really carefully in the future, slow things down and not be at someone's beck and call so much. If Adam called me in the middle of the night and wanted to come over, I wouldn't question it. I even used to make sure I'd have some beers in for him! In my last two failed relationships I forgot who I was and went on some kind of autopilot trying to be the world's best girlfriend, but really I just ended up as a doormat.

I dropped all of my friends both times too and would never make any plans just in case 'he wanted to see me'. On the occasions when I did go out with the girls, I'd leave early to get back for him, spend loads of time texting him and generally dominating the conversation with tales of my love life. God knows how and why my friends put up with it. I was just floating along on this cloud of infatuation and certainly wasn't being myself. But I wasn't being true to myself either. The second time I was dumped I had already experienced the feelings of disappointment, rejection, anger and bitterness, so I knew how to deal with it. I actually bounced back incredibly quickly and I know that I won't let myself get into the same situation again.

My friends have been amazing and say they are so happy that they've got 'the real me' back again. If anything good has come out of the situation it's a real sense of determination and power.

DATING DATA – POINTS TO REMEMBER
LEARNING LESSONS FROM THE PAST

→ Remember that everyone is different.
→ Do not put the blame on either your ex or yourself – analyse at which point the relationship started to fail.
→ See if you can spot any similar instances that have been repeated in your past relationships.
→ Create a relationship map or a picture of how you want to feel as a blueprint for future dating.

→ Don't try and hit the dating scene or go hunting for a new relationship if you are still really hung up and upset over your last one.

→ Don't try to be someone that you're not.

→ Take relationships slowly. If it's moving too fast, put the brakes on.

→ Dating and relationships should be enjoyable, if they're not, then do something about it!

3 WHERE ARE YOU NOW?

Your life at the moment and the emotional, physical, practical and economic reasons why you want to date. Plus, why your current lifestyle may be holding you back.

Before you start embarking on the big world of the dating scene, ask yourself what you personally want to get out of it. There's no point diving headlong into something without really working out why you're doing it, as it could be a recipe for more disaster. If you go and put yourself in a situation where you're likely either to get chatted up by someone or pick up someone without really thinking what you ultimately want from the experience, you could be asking for trouble. For example, you may go to a club and end up with a one-night stand, which may be fun at the time, but may ultimately leave you feeling lonelier than you were in the first place. Most of us singletons have been in the situation where we've had a couple of drinks (or more) and thought 'sod it, why not?' only to feel used/cheap/embarrassed/confused/or a combination of other uncomfortable feelings when we wake up the next day – whether or not we're with 'the mistake' from the night before.

Whether you spend an awkward evening in small talk or a night of unbridled passion, if it isn't what you wanted in the first place, you'll only feel worse about the situation afterwards. Worse still, you could be bulldozed into a relationship that you don't really want with someone who you might even just feel a bit sorry for, but feel that you might as well go along with, just in case it ends up being a good idea. And then both of you could end up getting hurt. A friend of mine who will remain nameless went out with someone for two years and recently admitted to me that she never fancied him; she thought he was a nice enough person but never enjoyed having sex with him. Sometimes she'd just fantasise it was Brad Pitt she was making love to. The two of them went on holiday, met each other's parents and just drifted along until he actually called it a day. They broke up totally amicably and they're still friends, but there was never anything in it. They were both at a stage in their lives where they fancied going out with someone and they were just in the right place at the right time.

With any kind of relationship you don't need to suck it and see (excuse the phrase if it has other connotations for you) – you should be in control of your own situation. You may not be able to call all the shots, but you can certainly work out what you want to get out of dating, so that you can put the brakes on if it doesn't go according to plan. If you just want to get into dating and see lots of people without any kind of commitment, fine. Similarly, if you want to go out there and search for a soulmate, that's what you should do. But first take a good look at your life at the moment. . .

You've established that you don't want to be single and that you'd like to be dating and generally more 'out there' in terms of romance, but what do you hope to gain out of a relationship and dating generally? It could be any number of emotional, physical, practical or even economic reasons. Personally, I want someone to wake up next to on a Saturday morning and make me a cup of tea (if only I could train my cat to do it). Another single male friend of mine wants someone to go on holiday with so that he isn't mistaken as homosexual when he's lying on a sun-lounger next to his mate – as if that really is a problem anyway. The point is, it's a personal reason but there are several reasons why you might want to be with someone at this time of your life.

Emotional reasons are probably the easiest to pinpoint. Feeling lonely is the most common reason why people don't want to be single, especially when it seems that everyone around us is happily loved-up and paired off. And while everyone else is busy planning their fabulous bank holidays, you're in a panic about how you're going to fill that extra day and wondering if there may be any fellow single people around to hook up with.

Saturday nights, holidays, attending weddings and other special occasions. . . these are just some of the times when you might want to be half of a couple to share and enrich experiences. Just getting home after a bad day at work and wanting to have someone to chat to and generally act as your sounding board is enough reason to hate being single.

You see couples in the supermarket choosing deliciously indulgent food together and you start fantasising about cosy dinners cuddled up in front of the TV or dinner parties with other 'equally fabulous' friends. In reality, of course, it's not all roses around the door and those loved-up couples may be just as frustrated as you are. But when you're single you can't help thinking that the grass is always greener on the other side. First of all, do yourself a favour and treat yourself to something deliciously indulgent the next time you are in the supermarket. Why should you miss out just because you're single? Don't make yourself feel any worse for heaven's sake. Secondly, the grass may look greener but appearances can be very deceptive. For all you know, that happy loving couple may be at each other's throats 90 per cent of the time. It's your life that you should be interested in, not that supposedly perfect couple's.

'MY BETTER HALF'

If it's not just feeling lonely, you may want to be part of a couple to boost other aspects of your emotional life, for example shortfalls in your personality. You may be lacking in confidence or find it difficult to hold your own in a conversation and would like the prop of a more confident partner. You may have other emotions to cope with, for example insecurity, depression or low self-esteem and feel that a partner or at least an occasional date would make certain scenarios in life easier to handle. If you identify with any of those personality traits it's important to understand that having a relationship, or even just a bit of a glamorous arm accessory, isn't automatically going to make life better. In fact it can make it even worse as it can confound all of those feelings of insecurity and move you even further down the emotional ladder. Nobody feels 100 per cent on top of things all the time and you can't expect anyone else to be your backbone.

You may believe that a trouble shared is a trouble halved and that if you had someone to offload your problems on to, everything would be fine. But you have to understand that everyone has their own degree of emotional baggage to handle, so don't go into any kind of relationship thinking that it's a tried-and-tested route to emotional happiness for both of you. It isn't. It takes a lot of work for relationships to work on an emotional level. The physical side can be a pushover compared to matters of the heart.

Of course relationships can be wonderfully supportive and there are people who truly believe they have found their soulmates, but it's a tough goal to set yourself, as American sociologist Pepper Schwartz explains. 'I firmly believe that soulmates exist, but then again I also believe in gold mines – and I know how hard it is to find one of them! If you base the whole of your life on just looking for a soulmate then you're going to find it tricky finding time to make a living! But because soulmates are as common as gold mines they get elevated to a Hollywood level and it's seen as the most romantic thing in the world for someone to find and get together with their soulmate. Therefore people choose to believe that they could never possibly find their soulmate through such mundane avenues as dating agencies or a dotcom programme. Soulmates aren't supposed just to fall out of the sky that way.'

Whether or not you do find your soulmate, via the 'Hollywood' ideal of a chance meeting in a bookshop or at the top of the Empire State Building or by giving fate a helping hand and being more proactive about finding someone, you are much more likely to be able to solve your own emotional problems yourself. Perhaps by means of self-assessment, talking things over with your close friends and if necessary having some kind of counselling, rather than assuming a boyfriend/girlfriend will have all the answers. Similarly, you shouldn't be expected to be able to provide all of the answers for a partner's emotional hang-ups. Some people end up being a kind of unpaid analyst or amateur counsellor for their partner. Sharing feelings is part of forming relationships, but it shouldn't be the sole reason for wanting to find a date or, ultimately, a mate.

Bound up with your emotional needs is what you physically want to get out of a relationship. Whether it's a reassuring hug at the end of the day, a little chat with your sweetheart over the phone or a full-blown sexual relationship, it's usually easy to work out what you feel your life lacks. If you have a very close family or lots of close friendships, you may have constant hugs and physical reassurance. But if the nearest thing you get to a cuddle is your cat landing on your bed in the middle of the night, then it's understandable that you feel you're missing out! You might just be envious of a couple you know who always hold hands as they walk along the street. That kind of physical affection can speak volumes of how special a relationship is.

On a more basic level, if you're crawling up the walls and craving sex for sex's sake, then that too is easy to identify. If masturbation doesn't light your fire and you crave physical closeness with someone else every night, or even just fancy the occasional shag, then it's an easy need to identify and acknowledge. Once you're in the position to verbalise what you want (but it's probably not such a good idea to shout it from the rooftops) you can then make better judgements about how you are going to tackle dating, what you want to get out of it and very importantly, what you can offer someone else. Remember, whether it's a blind date or a full-on relationship, there's more than one party involved and you should respect what the other person hopes to get out of the situation, as well as ticking off your own list of dating requirements.

FULFILLING ROLES

As politically incorrect as it may sound, many people want to get into a relationship because they ultimately want a husband or a wife to do the things they don't want to or can't do. They might not want to admit it, but there are plenty of blokes who'd like a wife automatically to take on the ironing, cooking and cleaning and be a kind of mum to them. And there are plenty of females out there who are happy to say that gardening, DIY and car maintenance are firmly the man's domain or a husband's job description – not their own.

You may have very practical reasons for wanting to find a partner as well as the fact that you'd like to have someone around to love. Maybe you can't drive and you have no intention of learning to, or perhaps you have children from a former relationship that you need support with? Four hands are certainly better than two when it comes to doing the daily chores. Economically things may be tough on your own and two salaries would obviously be better than one in your household, if only you could find the right person with a six-figure salary who'd like to move in. Or you can see how much better the quality of your life could be if you could share a mortgage or invest in something as a partnership. It can be a purely financial reason for wanting to meet someone, but there is a lot of emotion wrapped up with any kind of relationship, so tread carefully.

If you're looking for someone purely as an emotional prop, then you have to ask yourself if someone else is really going to make you feel secure. 'Probably not,' says Life Strategist, Pete Cohen. 'The only person who can make you feel secure is you yourself. A lot of people think their lives will be complete when they are in a relationship. But if you aren't comfortable with who you are at the outset, then you are going to struggle when you are in a relationship as your insecurities and your imperfections will come out further down the line.'

LIFE LAUNDRY DIARY

Whatever your reasons for wanting to date or find a relationship, once you've established what those reasons are, take a look at your lifestyle and consider why it could be holding you back. You don't have to approach this as if it's going to be your life's work, but one of the quickest ways of identifying a problem is to look at it on paper. For example, if you want to lose weight, the first step is to record your daily intake as a food diary (honestly, or it won't work). Then consider where you are going wrong and how you can make easy and effective changes. Similarly, write down your day-to-day activities. Your diary could look something like this:

MONDAY
Went to work
Ate my lunch at my desk
Came home
Watched TV
Went to bed

(through to. . .)
SATURDAY
Put a wash on
Went shopping
Saw a film with a friend
Came home, watched TV and had a takeaway delivered

There's nothing wrong with how you choose to fill your days, so don't beat yourself up if you choose to spend your weekends rearranging your sock drawer instead of white-water rafting. There will also be plenty of times when you enjoy the regular timetable of work, telly and bed. But unless you find yourself starring in a Meg Ryan movie, it's unlikely that you are going to meet a significant other in the kind of 9–5 weekday scenario above, unless you make some kind of effort to make things happen. Those chance meetings where you meet the love of your life at the water cooler at work only happen in chick flicks. So start playing out your life differently, even if it's something as simple as browsing around a bookshop at lunchtime or taking time out to do some kind of after-work activity. Whether it's joining a gym or meeting a friend for a coffee, reassessing your day-to-day life can only help. Even if you decide, at the end of the day, that you like your life the way it is after all.

Chapter 5 deals with widening your social circles, but before you get there you need to do your own life laundry to establish what you really want to get out of a relationship, and how much you yourself can offer another person. You may not realise it until you actually put it on paper, but an average day diary for you could be:

MONDAY
Went to work
Saw a friend for lunch
Went to my evening class
Late dinner, then bed

(through to. . .)
SATURDAY
Hung-over. Went to the gym
Went to visit Mum
Dinner with the girls

You may think that there's plenty of time in there to fit in a significant other – for example the two hours after the gym and when you have supper and watch TV before you collapse into bed and fall asleep three and a half seconds later. But if you actually look at your life from day to day, what with the gym, evening classes, friends that you see regularly, family commitments and, let's not forget, time that you need just for yourself, there may not be a whole lot left over. How is he/she going to fit in with the whole scheme of things? Would you put up with being very much a part-time hobby after a while? And remember you can only make time for someone else if first you make time for yourself, otherwise you'll be too frazzled to handle any kind of relationship.

You may have very definite ideas about how you would like to date – see a selection of people for a few dates, then start to see someone more seriously and go on from there. Or you may just want to meet Mr/Ms Right and not bother with people who don't fit your criteria. Alternatively you may just want a better social life and someone to share it with on a very ad-hoc basis. (The idea of a serious 'happy ever after' relationship may fill you with terror!) You may change your mind further down the line, but if you have some kind of idea about what you want to get out of a relationship you're less likely to waste (sometimes very precious) time and cause yourself and other people heartache.

DESIGN A DATE

Pete Cohen suggests that you should create a picture in your head of the sort of relationship you want to have. 'You don't have to work at it,' he says, 'just keep a picture of yourself with someone who you can laugh with and have a good time with. Then just go out and keep going on dates until you come across that person. It's a big pill to swallow but people should really try not to put too much into a relationship from the word go. Instead why not just have a good time? I've met people who have gone on dates and the person inside their heads is talking to them and saying, "Nice shoulders and probably quite good in bed and oh, his hair is falling out though. . ." And they are constantly talking to themselves about the person or panicking about what the other person is thinking about them. Forget about it. Just enjoy it. Don't think about from here to eternity, just think about this moment because it's all you've got. This moment is the future and people forget that. It's like people who save up a pension all their lives and then only have two years to spend it. If you are going on a date and you are thinking about the next date and the date after that, how many kids you are going to have and what you are going to wear at the wedding – what are you doing? Try not to have a picture of five kids and a house with a picket fence around the edge, just think of finding some fun and happiness from a relationship, better still a great friendship.'

HOW TO FIND HIM/HER

Once you've established what you want from a relationship, you can decide whether you would like the occasional ego-boosting date or a full-on romance and can then go about finding the person you'd like to meet. It stands to reason that people who just want to have a bit of fun, a frivolous flirtation or just a meaningless commitment-free shag are likely to be found in fun places – bars, parties, clubs and all of the usual 'chat up' venues. Where you go on holiday will also determine the kind of people who you are likely to meet. It stands to reason that you wouldn't meet the same crowd clubbing in Ibiza as you would on a reading weekend in Hay-on-Wye. OK, maybe you know the exception, but you get the drift. . .

Someone who is looking for a more serious relationship is probably more likely to use a no-nonsense approach like a dating agency. Of course, the lines are blurred and you can equally meet someone who is looking for their Mr/Ms Right in the local pub as you can find someone who wants to date plenty of different partners by using a dating agency.

Scanning a selection of lonely-hearts ads you can quickly see the difference in people's preferences, from 'seeking laughter and fun' to 'seeking lasting/loving relationship', or 'seeking soulmate for good times' to 'excursions, candlelight and cuddles'. It's up to you to go with the flow until you can establish what you and your potential date/long-term mate want out of the situation. There are no hard and fast rules, but there are ways to avoid the pitfalls and steer yourself in better directions to get the results that you want. Remember that you can be in control of the situation from the word go. You won't be able to dictate every move of the relationship, but you can keep checking back to what you actually want out of any arrangement. In that way you are less likely to be swept along in a direction that you don't really want to go in. Take the reins and continually remind yourself of your goal, keep tabs on whether you are heading in the right direction and re-route accordingly. Don't ever let anyone tell you that you are too old to change certain aspects of your life. If something is making you unhappy, find a way to make it better.

CASE STUDY

Gemma, 32, a marketing assistant from Suffolk, has realised that she has a much richer social life when she is single than when she is in relationships.

I used to fill my diary up for weeks in advance with things to do almost every night and definitely every weekend. If I didn't know on the Monday what I'd be doing on the Saturday it would fill me with panic and I'd be on the phone organising things with my other single friends and my family. It was a kind of security blanket for not having a boyfriend. When I was younger and went out with people I'd consciously not plan anything so that we could be spontaneous and just go with the flow, but I just can't do that as a single person. It scares me that I'll be on my own on a Saturday night with no prospect of anything to do on the Sunday either. I have to have a real structure to my life. I go to the gym at least three times a week after work and I have Italian classes every Wednesday, so that leaves me with Friday night when I usually go to the pub with my work mates and then the weekends when I see my friends. The trouble is we're all knackered by the time it comes to the weekend, so we usually just go around each other's houses and moan about never meeting anyone, rather than making an effort and doing something different. Or else we'll end up in some cattle market of a pub flirting for flirting's sake or having a one night stand, which never seems to end up anywhere. You just end up feeling embarrassed the next morning and a bit sick when you realise who you took home with you.

It's been three years since my last serious relationship but I recently thought I'd met 'the one' who was actually someone that I'd known for years. I didn't fancy him at all but I really threw myself into the relationship because I really thought it was what I wanted. But seeing that I was busy nearly every weekday night and at least one of the nights at the weekend, it was a very slow burner. I thought that he would find the idea of a very loosely structured relationship quite cool and it would give him time to see his friends and have his own hobbies. But it didn't really go to plan though as he wasn't prepared to organise his life around the free nights I had for him and I wasn't prepared to cancel anything to fit in around him, so it was stalemate really. When either of us tried to push for something more in the relationship, the other person resisted it – almost as if it was about keeping the upper hand. I then realised that I wasn't having half as much fun with him as I was when I was out with my friends and although he had everything going for him as a boyfriend, I couldn't see it going anywhere as a relationship.

I wasn't prepared just to let my very structured life dissolve in case the relationship didn't work out with him, leaving me in one of those voids that I used to find so frightening. Now that I'm so engrossed in my own life I know I'll find it difficult to allow anyone else to be part of it although I don't want to be on my own – crazy isn't it? Casual dating works for me because I like flirting and the occasional bit of romance, but unless I meet someone who'll fit around my schedule it's unlikely to blossom into anything else. I know it's unlikely that I'll meet someone who can be so 'casually committed' but the important thing for me is to do what makes me happy – and if that means a packed diary and the occasional flirtation than that's a lot more like a fulfilled life than just being at someone else's beck and call.

DATING DATA – POINTS TO REMEMBER
WHERE ARE YOU NOW?

→ Ask yourself what you want to get out of dating – several one-off relationships that may lead to something permanent or a one-way ticket to meeting Mr/Ms Right?

→ Establish the reasons why you want to date. Ask yourself whether it's for emotional, physical, practical, financial or any other reasons.

→ Keep a diary of your life as it is at the moment and work out why it's currently stopping you from dating.

→ Ask yourself if you really have time for someone else or whether you just want to improve your social life.

→ Consider whether you actually keep enough time for yourself.

→ Make a picture in your head of what you'd like to get out of a relationship and plan your relationship offensive.

4 CONFIDENCE BUILDING

General self-assertiveness, learning from people-watching and identifying windows for conversation.

You can't put your finger on quite what it is, but it's the easiest thing in the world to spot if someone is desperate to be in a relationship. It's a whole package of emotions, body language, vocabulary and a clumsy demeanour that seems to scream, *'I'm lonely, I hate it and I need someone now!'* From the way you hold yourself – shoulders forward, head down – to the way your eyes seem to plead for affection, clutching at straws of opportunity and clinging on to suggestions of romance. Take two girlfriends: one single, one 'attached' and it's easy to spot who's the single one. Even if she is very confident and seems to have a sassy attitude to life, if she is desperate to be in a relationship she will leak clues by her answers to questions and her reactions to talking about relationships.

Being desperate is not sexy, it's not appealing and it doesn't do anybody any favours. True, you might get the odd sympathy snog or shag because, quite honestly, you look as though you're gagging for it, but whoever you get together with is unlikely to stick around because the pressure from you will be too intense. Even if you do form some kind of relationship you'll be walking on eggshells to keep it afloat. One false move or one clingy comment too many and another relationship will bite the dust.

FALL IN LOVE

So how do you shake off the air of desperation and take on some kind of superhero status? It's all about positive thinking. It may sound like a cliché, but if you start loving yourself then others will fall for you too. Confidence and strength are incredibly sexy (as long as those characteristics don't turn into arrogance) and once you have the body language basics off pat and start to truly believe in yourself, then you're on the right track.

'If you want to start being confident you have to start imagining how you would be if you were confident,' says Pete Cohen. 'How would a confident person stand, how would you feel about yourself? Write yourself a little script of how you would go out and chat someone up. Then practise it in front of a mirror. You don't have to get it right first time – it's not opening night – you can keep playing around with it until you're an actor of whatever you want to be.'

Of course, it's difficult even to play at being confident if you are totally depressed and feel as though you have had all of the stuffing knocked out of you in too many relationships before. But sometimes you have to file your emotions away for a while and try focusing on something completely different. Here, Pete suggests another type of visualisation. 'Colour is a wonderful thing to use. If you focus on yellow, and feel that yellow is being pumped into your body, completely filling you up from your toes and your heart and bones and skin and muscles and every cell of your body, it will really brighten you up inside. Try it now.

'Depressed people know that they're good at being depressed. The thing to do is to ask yourself if you want to carry on being depressed. Yes or no? I find that many depressed people don't want to change because it's too much of a personal investment to do so. People act out the part of someone who is depressed or shy and they won't even attempt to change themselves – it's too much of an effort.' You have to make a conscious decision to get to grips with your depression. Clinical depression is naturally a much bigger issue than just being a bit fed up, in which case your GP will be able to advise you on the best action for you personally to take. But even identifying that you have some kind of depression will help you on the road to recovery. It sounds simplistic, but it's a matter of deciding whether you want to continue being depressed or not and some people actually feed off their own depression.

FACE YOUR FEARS

Dating and new people can be very daunting. Everyone gets nervous about meeting people sometimes. Even world leaders probably get the collywobbles when they meet each other and know what's potentially at stake. It's totally natural. Whether you are going for a job interview or contemplating chatting someone up at a bar, you get nervous because you recognise the potential for failure before you've even come face to face with someone. 'Nervousness comes around,' says Pete, 'because very simply you are talking to yourself too much. If a man goes into a room and he sees a beautiful woman on the other side of the bar, he might think, I'm going to go and talk to her. But straight away he'll hear a voice inside his head saying "don't be stupid, she won't like you" and the woman gets stronger and stronger until she ends up looking like an Amazonian giant! No wonder it's terrifying. It's the same with fears and phobias. If I did what an agoraphobic did, I'd never go out of the house.' The more you tell yourself how badly things could go wrong, the more you convince yourself that something is a bad idea in the first place.

The tried and tested way to deal with many phobias is to think, 'What's the worst thing that could happen?' In the case of the man at the bar, the woman could tell him where to go. If that's the case and that's the type of woman she is then who'd want to know her anyway? When you start talking to yourself in this way, you annihilate problems. The fear of what could possibly happen is always going to be stronger than the outcome. 'It's like a little duck quacking away in your psyche,' says Pete. 'You have to say, shut the duck up! If you keep thinking, what if this happens, and then this and oh, this. . . it's a foregone conclusion that you'll stress yourself out. You've just got to stop listening to those negative thoughts.'

LEARN FROM OTHERS

Turn on the TV and see how some television presenters seem to exude confidence. The smile, the personality and the ease with which they get information across seems effortless. You feel that you could really get to know them because they seem so open, friendly and down to earth. With their heads held high and the ability to look someone straight in the eye they seem to be saying, 'I'm in control here, this is my show and this is how I want the outcome to be.' In a similar way, learn a few lessons from friends of yours that you also think are really confident – or 'people-watch' when you're next in a bar. Look at the package of emotions, body language and attitude. You don't even need to hear what someone is saying to see if they have a captive audience. And people don't need to be drop-dead gorgeous to have a magnetic personality or a natural charisma, it's all about what's going on inside their heads.

INSTANT SEX APPEAL

'If you want to go and talk to someone you fancy at a bar,' says Pete, 'think about what it was like the last time you were in love with someone and you just couldn't keep your hands off them. Even when you start thinking about it your pheromones come to life and a chemical reaction starts happening in your body. It works like nobody's business. And if you've never been in love, imagine what it feels like and imagine the pheromones you are giving off.

'Another thing you can do if you are shy is to make a sound like "Yee ha!" in your head. Or imagine you have your own inner coach like Madonna or Barry White and they're filling you with confidence and sex appeal. If those two don't work for you, think about someone who does. Give yourself a silent sense of power and start enjoying a situation for what it might be, rather than negatively talking yourself out of a potential opportunity. Recognise the worst thing that could happen in a situation and then tell yourself that you are mentally prepared for it and you'll be in control whatever happens.'

START TALKING

Feeling nervous about a situation is often caused by not knowing what to say. You feel that there is a lot riding on your opening words and that you could possibly do more harm than good by saying anything at all. A comedian said that he was so nervous about saying hello to a girl once that he opened his mouth and instead of saying hello he said, 'Beware!'

You may have convinced yourself that you feel confident enough about being in the same room or situation as someone else, but now what? How do you go about making the first move when you sense that the other person is unlikely to meet you halfway and that you'll miss out on an opportunity if you don't say something?

You can find windows for conversation in all sorts of situations. For example, if you really fancy someone that you see regularly in your local Blockbuster shop, go and ask his/her opinion of one of the latest releases – but steer clear of the pornography section, at least for the time being! British people are traditionally very conservative and distrustful of strangers – especially in big cities like London where there are so many crazy people around. Many men say they are very reticent to start talking to women in case they make them feel uncomfortable or threatened, so they back off entirely. It's therefore much easier for a woman to strike up a conversation with a man than the other way around. And men are so anxious about overstepping the mark that they sometimes miss really obvious come-ons from women! So it's stalemate all round.

PLAY TENNIS

Getting into a bit of chit-chat with someone is a little art form all of its own. It's all about playing conversational tennis and, depending on what kind of points you are aiming to score with the other person, you can miss the first stroke or have someone running around the court while you happily keep volleying information. Remind yourself that when you meet someone that you feel drawn to, you should think of them as being a potential new friend rather than a potential date/lover/wife/husband and so on. Conversation is the basis of all friendship, exchanging views and getting to know details about each other; it doesn't need to be high-brow, witty, intense or hard work. Start off talking about just about anything (avoid personal subjects) and see where it takes you.

There's always something to talk about, even if it's the weather (God help us). The hairdressers' favourite of 'have you been on holiday this year?' is a fairly innocuous way to start a conversation and you can find out a lot about them into the bargain. But whether it's a chat-up line or just passing conversation, if it's incongruous and your timing is completely out it will sound nerdy. Often, relationships don't get past the starting post because of clumsy introductions and crass chat-up lines: 'Get your coat, you've pulled', or 'Do you come here often?' should only be delivered with a great deal of forethought and irony. Saying something like 'I'm sure I've met you before' will always prompt some kind of response, even if it's 'No, you haven't,' in which case you can either say 'I'm so sorry,' and move on, or decide to try and work out where it was that you 'saw' him/her. You could say, 'Do you go to x [gym, bar, local beauty spot]?' By that time his/her body language will tell you whether they want to continue the conversation or whether you're wasting your time completely and should move away.

The important lesson is that you really have to take the bull by the horns sometimes. Take a leap into the unknown, realising that it could fail, but feeling empowered because you are doing something positive. Wishing and hoping and fantasising that something is miraculously going to happen is hopeless. In this day and age you have to make things happen for yourself, even if you are the most shy person on the planet. Remember that you can always try acting out the role of a confident person.

'It's what's behind what you say and the passion and the excitement that you have for life, rather than what you say,' says Pete Cohen. 'We're emotional transmitters and when we feel good inside that's what we transmit to other people. If you don't believe me, then go and hang out with a bunch of depressed people and see what happens after a few hours. The chances are you'll be depressed too. If you can feel good inside like you're wearing a big smile from one shoulder to the other shoulder and across your chest, you won't need to say very much, you'll just transmit signals and you won't have to work at conversations – they'll just happen.'

MAKE THEM LAUGH!

Using humour is a great way to strike up a conversation with someone, whether you are going for the full-on flirt, or just widening your social circles (see Chapters 7 and 8). It immediately relaxes people and puts them more at ease and takes the serious edge off a first encounter – as long as your opening gambit is genuinely witty and not offensive or sarcastic. You might be one of those people who think that you have the whole of the opposite sex sussed out, but remember everyone is different and people can react unexpectedly to so-called 'safe' subjects. It's sod's law that if you show interest in someone's family that they'll have had a recent bereavement, or that if you give someone a compliment they'll start wondering what your motives are. We humans are a very distrustful lot.

Self-deprecating comments work to a certain level, but be careful how far you go – especially if you are trying to chat someone up. Revealing personal details about your bodily functions or constantly putting yourself down is an instant turn-off. You are meant to be selling yourself to the other person, not driving them away. Chapter 9 deals with how you should go about describing yourself in a personals ad and the fact that you should never, ever put yourself down on paper. Face to face it's slightly different as both parties will be able to make judgements for themselves, but too often women think it's fine and quite funny to keep putting themselves down. The majority of women would never dream of being arrogant, but in terms of dating and forming romantic relationships, you won't be doing yourself any favours if you start slagging yourself off. You may be so convincing that the guy that you fancy believes all those horrible things you say about yourself.

ULTIMATE CHAT-UP LINES

Here's the bad news: unfortunately, there are no hard and fast 100 per cent guaranteed chat-up lines for every occasion which will help you hook a partner and reel them in. But once your confidence grows, you'll find you can smile naturally and talk to anyone – from the local librarian to Hollywood's hottest bachelor or bachelorette (spinster is such a brittle, unglamorous word). It's all a matter of assessing the situation and taking the plunge.

→ The first step is feeling confident – or at least having an inner voice working for you and refusing to listen to the negatives.
→ The second is knowing what could possibly go wrong with an encounter and being mentally prepared for the worst.
→ The third is putting a smile on your face, taking the plunge and saying hello.

There, how difficult was that? The alternative of course is to keep quiet, stay out of the action and just keep fantasising about what could have happened, if only you'd had more guts. Turn the tables on yourself for a change and see how good it feels.

CASE STUDY

Clara, now 41, met her husband using her favourite chat-up line and bags of confidence.

I was in a bar in Soho with my friend Julia and the two of us had both been drinking cocktails, so we were feeling very relaxed. We'd both just split up with long-term boyfriends and we were having the 'all men are crap' conversation. That didn't stop us from looking around though and there were some really nice guys in the bar that night as I think someone was having a leaving do. We'd both gone out for some retail therapy and I knew I was looking good. I'd had my hair done and I had this killer lipstick on and felt great. I decided that I'd try my favourite chat-up line which worked very well the last time I tried it and I walked up to this guy and said, 'Hello, you're gorgeous.' He grinned this massive grin and said, 'So are you,' and that was that. We spent the whole evening talking and he introduced me to his mate as 'This is Clara, the woman I'm going to marry.' Six weeks later we moved in together and got engaged less than six months after the day we'd met. I quickly became pregnant and this year I had our third child. It's been an amazing relationship and best of all, we both still fancy each other like mad.

I'm not confident about everything in life, but I knew on the night I met Johnnie that it was the thing to say. And it worked. I've told other friends of mine to try it and it nearly always works for them too. I suppose you have to have the balls to pull it off, but what have you got to lose?

DATING DATA – POINTS TO REMEMBER
CONFIDENCE-BUILDING

→ Think about how positive people act and practise in front of a mirror.
→ If you are feeling depressed, try and make a conscious decision to get to grips with your depression.
→ Understand the worst-case scenario of a situation so that you are mentally prepared for the potential outcome.

→ Copy confident people's actions.
→ Will yourself to feel more confident inside.
→ Look for 'windows' of conversation and use humour if you can.
→ Keep conversation light and impersonal.
→ Dare yourself to do something different sometimes.

5 FLIRTING AND BODY LANGUAGE

From the subliminal to the downright obvious: how to spot if someone is interested in you and how you can flirt more successfully.

Not only is it great fun to flirt and be flirted with, but anthropological research shows that it is a basic instinct and part of human nature. Let's face it, if nobody flirted or showed any interest in the opposite sex, humans wouldn't be around for much longer. Therefore, anthropologists define flirting as 'a natural courtship ploy that has been evolved to attract and keep sexual partners doing what comes naturally'. That's the scientific definition anyway. In practice it can be an incredible adrenalin-pumped endorphin rush and done successfully it can be more sexy than foreplay.

Like every aspect of dating, flirting has its own set of unwritten laws and etiquette to follow, which state how, when, where and with whom we can flirt. The rules get broken when someone throws a spanner in the works – like when he/she flirts with someone inappropriate, says something crass or crashes in with chat-up lines before they have evaluated whether the time is right or not. It doesn't matter who you speak to about flirting, whether it's your best friend who seems to have the gift of the gab or the world's greatest anthropologists with conclusive data, flirting and body language can be evaluated in a number of different ways. . .

SMOOTH TALKING

In 1997 the Society for Human Sexuality (yes there really is such a thing) held a flirting forum. They described the art of flirting as 'casual conversation with a romantic spark' and it was agreed that it is a skill that could be learned – which is lucky for those of us who perceive successful flirting as being about as easy as canoeing up Niagara Falls. Various techniques were discussed in precise scientific detail at the forum but it was agreed that the framework for any kind of flirting session needed to include the following:

→ Make sure you ask specific, open-ended questions about the person that you are flirting with, i.e. not just yes or no answers. This not only increases your knowledge of the person, it's a great form of flattery and provides an opportunity for the discussion to take a romantic turn.
→ Look for humour in what the person is saying and let yourself laugh at his or her jokes (if you find them funny). Again, it's very flattering for the person who is delivering the lines and it will make you both feel more at ease.
→ Try to look your best and use good posture and eye contact.
→ Don't follow people around or act needy. (Remember those rules about giving off 'desperate and dateless' vibes.)
→ Try not to be insincere (even though you may feel as though you're standing at the edge of a cliff with no safety rope).

The forum concluded that once you have all of the basics in place, you can then assess whether someone is interested in you. Some clues that will help you are:

→ If he or she is acting more flirtatiously towards you than towards other people at the same event/in the same place.
→ If his or her friends are paying attention to you and engaging you in conversation when he or she isn't around. This is often a big clue that the person talked to his or her friends about you.
→ If he or she is smiling while listening to you and seems to be listening especially 'actively'. Obviously, flirting isn't the only time that you listen to someone intently, people concentrate on others' conversation all the time, but it's the 'romantic spark' that distinguishes it from the normal good listening.

So much for the framework, but how do you find the right opportunity, who should you flirt with and how can you pull it off successfully?

WHERE TO FLIRT?

In theory, you can flirt anywhere. You don't have to be at a party or bar to flutter your eyelashes and come out with a sexy one-liner. In fact, the greatest flirts will never really stop flirting. The way that some people carry themselves and the aura that they seem to give off seems to shout 'come and get me, I'm a love machine!' They seem to flirt with their friends, strangers and have a natural confidence. For them there's a very fine line between flirting with someone and just being friendly and, sometimes, only they'll know the difference.

In practice, however, many people find it easier and more effective to flirt at places were flirting is expected (such as parties) and they'll only flirt then with the help of alcohol. According to a flirting survey carried out by the drinks company Martini, alcohol was voted the most effective aid to flirting, with 27 per cent of couples meeting their current partner in a pub. But it's not just down to alcohol – the way that a pub is laid out can really help or hinder flirting opportunities. Many pubs have a very public zone around the bar and more private areas such as booths, tables and chairs, therefore the mere fact of positioning yourself in one of these public or private zones means that you are indicating your social mood. You may be secretly hoping that someone will come over to the far corner of the pub where you are sitting and chat you up, but it's actually highly unlikely that anybody would make such a bold move as there are unwritten rules about flirting zones. The fact that you have positioned yourself there subliminally says that you want to be away from prying eyes and prefer to be more of a 'watcher' than watched. Stand at the bar, however, and your chances double.

JOIN IN – OR ELSE!

With social occasions such as parties, weddings and other functions, flirting is almost part of the social etiquette – a way of letting your hair down and being more open to meeting new people. According to another scientific body, the Social Issues Research Centre in Oxford, refusal to join in with the expected amount of flirting at parties may actually cause disapproval, possibly from the host or perhaps other guests who think of it as just something you are supposed to do. Most parties and celebrations are governed by a special code of behaviour which anthropologists call 'cultural remission'. This means that a deliberate relaxation of normal social controls takes place and you are given an invisible licence to be able to increase the friendly-factor – as long as you don't break the flirting rules (see above). Just as parties encourage a light-hearted approach to confidence and more of a willingness to mix and be friendly to others, it's also OK to have a bit of a flirt.

WHO YOU REALLY SHOULD BE FLIRTING WITH

There are some very mismatched couples in the world but research proves that most successful marriages and long-term relationships are between partners who are more or less equally good looking. Which of course isn't great news for those among us who haven't been blessed with, let's say, 'traditional' good looks. There's no rule in the world that says you can't have a flirt with the supermodel in the corner of the room, but statistically, science tells us, where one partner is more attractive than the other, relationships are less successful. That's what science says – don't shoot the messenger if you don't agree.

Unfortunately, sizing up your own attractiveness is very difficult – especially as so many women have a poor body image. Because of our aesthetically obsessed culture, it's thought that up to 80 per cent of all adult women believe they are too fat. On the other hand, men tend to be far less critical, maybe because beauty ideals are not enforced so rigidly. Furthermore, men tend to overestimate how good looking they are and lack the subtleties of successful flirting. Therefore a less confident man with a better understanding of flirting skills could actually win the day over a cocky rival. Whether it leads to anything long-term of course is another question.

THE IMPORTANCE OF BODY LANGUAGE

You may have the complete gift of the gab but unwittingly your body language may be completely contradicting what you are saying. Experts have calculated that 55 per cent of the message that we get from someone comes through our body language, 38 per cent is from the tone, speed and inflection of our voice and just 7 per cent is from what we are actually saying. World famous anthropologist Charles Darwin first recognised the importance of body language in 1872 in his heavy-duty scientific study *The Expression of the Emotions in Men and Animals* and the subject has continued to fascinate people-watchers who have been able to crack the code of the body's gestures and movements.

It doesn't matter what nationality someone is, body language is basically the same for all humans. There are gestures that have unique meanings to certain cultures, but by reading several messages at once that the body is communicating, it is possible to interpret their hidden meaning. Allan Pease, author of *Body Language, How to Read Others' Thoughts by Their Gestures*, says that in order to read people's thoughts by their actions we have to look at groups of actions or 'gesture clusters'. 'Gestures come in sentences and invariably tell the truth about a person's feelings or attitude.' He says that anyone can read body language. 'Turn down the sound on the television and try and understand what is happening by just watching the picture. By turning the sound up every five minutes, you will be able to check how accurate your readings are.'

Everything from the way that you shake hands with someone to the way that you cross your legs gives off signals. Most body language experts believe in the 'Rule of Four' (like Allan Pease's gesture clusters) which means that you should look for at least four body language signals which say the same thing before you can completely sum up their meaning. For example, if someone is scratching their head it may mean that they're lying about something, they could be uncertain about something, have forgotten something or maybe they just have an itchy head! Therefore you have to see what other movements and gestures are going on at the same time. All body language experts will tell you that you shouldn't try and judge what someone is thinking on the basis of one gesture alone.

HANDY HINTS

Open palms are associated with honesty, scratching the nose or covering the mouth can be a signal that someone is lying, having your arms folded tightly across the chest is seen as defensive and keeping your chin down is supposedly critical or hostile. Allan Pease says it is difficult to fake body language, but it is good to learn positive open gestures and eliminate gestures that may give out negative signals. It can also, of course, help enormously with your flirting techniques!

HOW TO FLIRT USING BODY LANGUAGE

FIRST IMPRESSIONS

Because only 7 per cent of what you actually say to people adds up to their first impression of you, there's not really a lot of point trying to come up with a killer one-liner that will impress the birds out of the trees. Body language is therefore the trigger to what happens next.

SHOW THAT YOU ARE INTERESTED

Instead of thinking up ways to impress someone, show that it's you that's impressed by him or her. If the object of your affection knows you find him/her interesting and/or attractive, they will be more inclined to be interested in you in return. They enjoy the attention and will want it to continue. On the other side of the coin, if someone starts showing that kind of interest in you, even if you don't fancy them to start off with, once you hear that they are interested in you, you may find that your interest in them automatically increases. Many people don't even consider someone as a potential partner until they discover that person fancies them. Suddenly you sit up and take notice because you are enjoying the attention.

EYE CONTACT

Your eyes are your most important flirting tool as they are high-powered emotion transmitters. Looking directly at someone can convey a whole spectrum of emotions from instant attraction to outright hostility. You may not have realised it but eye contact is so powerful that in normal circumstances, i.e. in everyday conversation, we generally avoid eye contact of more than one second with another person. Close friends, family and lovers are more comfortable about looking each other in the eye directly, but with strangers in public most people avoid any eye contact at all. The next time you are in a crowded environment like a bus or a very busy shop, see how people go out of their way to focus on inanimate objects instead of catching someone's eye.

TURN IT TO YOUR ADVANTAGE

If you find someone attractive and you feel that it's appropriate to flirt with that person (and they're not in the 'out of bounds' league) trying catching their eye for more than a second. If your target looks away immediately, then looks back briefly, then you can safely assume he/she is interested. And if there's a smile on his/her face too, then you're definitely on the right track. On the other hand, if you initiate the first look and he/she looks away and continues to look away, then you should read the signs that this may not be the great romance that you were hoping for. Of course, the other person could just be very shy, in which case you should try and see if he/she reacts to other people in the same way.

START TALKING!

Unwittingly, when we are having a conversation with someone, the person who is speaking often looks away from the person who is listening. The rule book says that to show interest when someone is talking to you, you should look at them directly in glances of between one and seven seconds. People often stare longingly at another person and hang on their every word, but this tends to make the other person feel uncomfortable, rather than appreciating their directness. But as you consciously move your eyes away, be careful where your eyes go when you are not looking someone directly in the eye – if a man starts talking directly to a woman's cleavage, it's likely to be a short conversation. And if you find yourself staring at a man's bald patch or a clump of hair growing out of his ears, it's unlikely to make him feel great about the encounter.

Someone told me a story about a friend of hers who spent an entire date with a huge piece of broccoli stuck in the middle of her front teeth. She'd spent the evening dancing around and smiling at everyone and hadn't really picked up on the strange looks she was getting. When she got home she was absolutely mortified that her date hadn't mentioned the vegetable addition to her smile. It would have been better for both of them if he'd casually said, 'I think you have something in your teeth.' Situations like that are not a big deal and being up-front can save a lot of embarrassment later.

KEEP YOUR DISTANCE

Personal space is very important, so experts tell us that we should avoid getting too close for comfort. Pay attention to how much space the other person puts between you and him/her and keep an invisible rule between you. According to Allan Pease, personal space can be divided up into four zones: Public, Social, Personal and Intimate. It's obvious that the Intimate Zone (15–46cm) should only be crossed by people you are very emotionally attached to such as family, lovers and very close friends. The Personal Zone (46cm–1.2m) can be crossed by people you are talking to on a social level – new friends, close colleagues and so on. The Social Zone (1.2–3.6m) is the space you'll probably prefer to keep between you and strangers (even though it's called the Social Zone, you don't really want to socialise with these people). Meanwhile the Public Zone (over 3.6m) is the distance people generally try to maintain if they are addressing an audience or a large gathering.

Of course it's difficult always to keep your distance with people. If you're on a packed train it's hard not to find yourself too close for comfort with an absolute stranger. But if you always consider people's personal space it will help them feel more comfortable with you. As far as flirting is concerned, initially do not cross that 46cm barrier and go closer than the Personal Zone. You don't have to take a tape measure with you everywhere you go, just check out what the distances actually equate to and keep a mental note for the future.

People may seem very friendly and inviting but you can undo all your positive social skills by getting too close to someone. Just because you may be a very touchy-feely person, it doesn't mean that everyone else is. Many women are very conscious of keeping someone 'at arm's length' until they feel comfortable enough to allow them any closer. My closest friend was filled with horror when I told her someone's dating story in this book. The girl in question met this guy who gave her a great big hug and my friend said, 'Oh no, that's terrible. I'd absolutely hate that. How dare he?' The moral of this story is don't assume that everyone has the same rules about getting close as you have.

Look out for 'barrier signals' from people such as crossed arms, crossed legs or rubbing their neck with the elbow pointed towards you. If you are also getting negative facial expressions it's definitely time to back off, whether you are male or female. If they're looking bored, yawning or looking around the room, do you really need to be told that you're not exactly on to a winner?

There are a great many variations in people's personal space preferences and even the same person can vary from day to day, so remember the 'rule of four' and look for sets of gestures that will help you read the meaning behind someone's body language.

MORE CLUES

Tracey Cox, author of *Supersex* and flirting coach of the BBC's *Would Like To Meet* series says there are five secret sexual signs that someone is flirting with you:*

1. THE FLIRTING TRIANGLE

When we look at people we're not close to (in a business situation for instance), our eyes make a zig-zag motion: we look from eye to eye and across the bridge of the nose. With friends, the look drops below eye level and moves into a triangle shape: we look from eye to eye but also look down to include the nose and mouth. Once we start flirting, the triangle gets even bigger – it widens at the bottom to include their good bits (like the body). The more intense the flirting, the more intensely we'll look from eye to eye – and the more time we'll spend looking at their mouth. If someone is watching your mouth while you're talking to them, it's very, very sexy because you can't help but think, 'I wonder if they're imagining what it would be like to kiss me.' Which is usually exactly what they are thinking, if they're looking intently at your mouth!

2. MIRRORING

This is what separates a good flirt from a great flirt: nothing will bond you more instantly or effectively than mirroring someone's behaviour. This simply means you do whatever it is they do. If they lean forward to tell you something intimate, you lean in to meet them. If they sit back to take a sip of their drink and look you in the eye, you take a sip of your drink and do the same. If they sit with their chin cupped in their hands, so do you.

*Adapted from the *Would Like To Meet* dating advice on www.bbc.co.uk/health/dating

The theory behind mirroring is that we like people who are like us. If someone is doing what we're doing, we feel they're on the same level as us and in the same mood as we are. Two no-nos with this one though: first up, only mirror positive body language; secondly, capture the spirit rather than imitating them like a chimpanzee at the zoo. As a general rule, wait around 50 seconds before following their gestures.

3. THE EYEBROW FLASH

When we first see someone we're attracted to, our eyebrows rise and fall. If they fancy us back, they raise their eyebrows in return. Never noticed? It's not surprising since the whole thing lasts about a fifth of a second!

We're not consciously aware of doing it, but it's a gesture that is duplicated by every culture on earth. In fact, some experts claim it's the most instantly recognised non-verbal sign of friendly greeting in the world. The trick is to watch for it when you meet someone new you fancy. Even better, tell them you're interested on a subconscious level by extending your eyebrow flash for up to one second – deliberately raise them while catching their eye for full impact.

4. POINTING

Sneak a peek at what their feet and hands are doing – we tend to point towards the person we're interested in. If we find someone attractive, we'll often point at them subconsciously with our hands, arms, feet, legs, toes. Again, it's an unconscious indicator to make our intentions known. Unconsciously, this is often picked up by the other person, without them really knowing why.

5. BLINKING

If someone likes what they see, their pupil size increases and so does their blink rate. If you want to add up the odds in your favour, try increasing the blink rate of the person you're talking to, by blinking more yourself. If the person likes you, they'll unconsciously try to match your blink rate to keep in sync with you, which in turn, makes you both feel more attracted to each other!

EARLY WARNING SIGNS

Just as there are signs that will tell you if someone is flirting with you, there are also signs that signal someone is not telling you the truth, which can make the difference between a happy relationship or another heartbreak:

→ **Look out for insincere smiles that don't quite reach the eyes. Real smiles make the eyes crinkle and fake smiles will make the face asymmetrical and they look exaggerated. If a smile stays in a fixed position for too long it's definitely being forced.**

→ **Learn to see a lie. It's difficult to look someone directly in the eye and lie convincingly. When a man rubs a closed eye vigorously while looking at the floor it's usually a sign that there's a lie behind the action (unless he's prone to allergies! Remember the rule of four!) Women on the other hand tend to massage the skin under the eye and look at the ceiling if they are fibbing. Evasion signs such as hiding palms, keeping hands behind the back or in pockets are all signals that the truth is being held back.**

TURN FLIRTING INTO AN ART FORM!

Peta Heskill runs a Flirting Academy devoted to helping you become 'more wonderful, more confident and more able to flirt – not just with people, but with *LIFE*!' On her website www.flirtcoach.com you can read and download articles, quizzes, motivational quotes such as 'a compliment a day keeps the frowns away' and details of her flirting courses which are held four times a year in London, plus her unique 'dating, mating and relationship coaching programme'.

Peta says one of the most important components of successful flirting is being in the right mood. 'Good flirts are playful, have a sense of fun, adventure and a curiosity about people. Instead of worrying whether you will score or make a good impression with someone, focus on what you can give. See how easily you can make the other person feel good.' Sigmund Freud said 'we leak the truth from every pore' and Peta reiterates how important it is to be yourself. 'Phoneys get discovered sooner or later. If you pretend to be what you're not, you will very quickly find yourself with fewer friends, fewer connections and fewer opportunities to meet someone who is right for you.'

With all flirting techniques, some will work for you while others won't, so don't give up if you don't get immediate results. 'When you believe that there is no failure in life and that whatever result you get is a learning tool, you will succeed.'

Get a friend to tell you (honestly) what they think of your flirting technique. I've tried this with friends and apart from being a really good laugh it's actually a real eye opener and you can learn all sorts of tricks. One of my friends always wears a necklace which ends just where her cleavage begins. She fiddles with the necklace intermittently and just watches guys coming out in a sweat. Now you may not want to do something as overtly sexual as that, but your friend will at least be able to tell you what he/she thinks are your best physical qualities and what you should be making more of. One of my friends wears glasses and almost hides behind them. She'll wear lipstick and show off her mouth but she forgets that she has beautiful eyes behind her glasses and that an occasional eyelash flutter wouldn't go amiss. She is, of course, fluttering them for Britain now.

CASE STUDY

Susie, 39, has always found flirting easy and one night met her match.

I was in a bar with my friends from work one Friday night and I met the brother of the receptionist from work who was absolutely jaw-droppingly gorgeous. It was lust at first sight. Feeling emboldened by vodka and knowing that I looked OK (well, actually I thought I looked pretty great that night) I started making eye contact with him and letting the straw in my drink linger just a little bit as I looked at him and the sparks began to fly. We were both so subtle about it and it was so exciting because I just knew that we would be getting together at some stage and so we spent at least an hour just looking at each other and sharing a private unspoken joke.

Finally, when I was just about to scream with frustration, he came over and this was the conversation:

Him: Is this the office local then?
Me: Would you like it to be?

Him: Do you always answer a question with a question?
Me: Not always. Do you?
Him: That depends. What would you like to happen next?
Me: I'm easy. The question is, are you?
Him: I couldn't say. How about buying me a drink and we'll discuss it?
Me: Isn't the man supposed to buy the drinks?
Him: Is this our first row?

Then at that stage I just started laughing and he did too. I introduced myself properly and yes, I did buy him a drink, but he bought me plenty of drinks after that and for the next five months that we were together. From the word go it was an incredibly flirtatious relationship. Unfortunately flirting was a bit of a drug to him and once our 'honeymoon' period was over he found another flirting partner. He used to do this thing where he'd touch the back of his top front teeth (which were lovely) with his tongue and then he'd grin this amazingly sexy grin. It never failed. Unfortunately our relationship did, but it was great fun at the time!

DATING DATA – POINTS TO REMEMBER
BODY LANGUAGE AND FLIRTING

→ Make sure you're in the right mood to flirt.
→ Look for gesture clusters in body language that 'say' the same thing.
→ Show that you are interested in the person you want to flirt with, rather than trying to impress them.
→ Use eye contact cleverly. Practise the flirting triangle and the eyebrow flash.
→ Keep your distance and don't invade someone's personal space – unless invited to.
→ Try mirroring a person's body language – but remember, not like a chimp.
→ Keep an eye open for defensive signs such as crossed arms and legs.
→ Read warning signs and back off if necessary.
→ Remember, some techniques will work for you and others won't. Persevere and put positive and negative results down to experience.

6 WIDENING YOUR SOCIAL CIRCLES

Making the most of environments that encourage interaction, identifying types of people and where you are likely to find them.

If you're one of those people who constantly moans 'I never meet anyone' or 'my friends and I always do the same thing' then it's no wonder you feel like a hamster stuck in a wheel, trundling through life doing the same thing week in, week out. It's only by making a very conscious decision to do different things and make changes in your life that you'll make different things happen to you. From the smallest things like sitting in a café at lunchtime with a book and a sandwich instead of eating your sandwich behind your desk, you'll be making an effort to make yourself more of a social animal. It will give you more confidence to go on making bigger moves and get yourself out of the rut that you may be stuck in.

Remember, your social life isn't up to fate, it's up to you and all that's stopping you from changing your life as it stands at the moment is you. Stop blaming it on friends (or lack of), your family commitments or any of the subconscious 'comfort zones' that you use as excuses for not getting out and meeting new people. There really is so much opportunity out there for single people. Start looking and asking around and you'll be amazed at how many social activities are designed for single people of all ages and in all walks of life. What's more, you don't have to go it alone, you can get together with another single mate so the whole thing isn't quite so daunting.

PEOPLE-SPOTTING

It will soon become clear to you (if it isn't already) what types of people are to be found in certain scenarios. So in order to find the man/woman who you think you would like to meet, you'll need to adjust your social life accordingly (and also perhaps your wardrobe). Equally, if you find that you are always meeting similar types, then you should try to do something radically different to embrace other potential personalities. Remember, it's only by breaking out of the rut that you are in that you are likely to move yourself forward. Go on, be daring. What's the worst thing that can happen?

DATING LOCATION: SUPERMARKET SINGLES' NIGHTS

People types: Busy local people just like you. They may be divorced, newly single, have children or a menagerie of pets – just check out the contents of their trolley for more clues.

You may say that the area that you live in isn't exactly conducive to romance, but it's up to you to do some digging around to find out what's out there waiting for you. Even going to the supermarket could be a potential for romance – especially if you happen to be wandering through the aisles at Asda in the week running up to Valentine's Day! Since 2000 the supermarket chain has held special singles' nights around Valentine's Day and other special holidays in all 250 of their UK stores, to encourage people to flirt while they shop. It's been a tremendous success in the north but not as successful in the south where shoppers are maybe more wary of wearing their green for 'go' or red for 'approachable but nervous' badges, or showing that they are open for a chat around the kitchen roll area.

According to Asda's resident Cupids who host the events, pairs of girls and boys seem to find the experience more rewarding as they feel there's safety in numbers. So you don't have to turn up on your own looking desperate and dateless, you could go along with a bunch of your single mates and have a browse at what's on offer! Asda's spokesperson Anna Smith says, 'We find that people have more chance of getting chatted up if they hang around the music and video sections. They're probably less likely to come face to face with their future love if they're buying a pound of sprouts!'

Like many dating initiatives, the idea of supermarket flirting originated in the United States, where many of the major stores have very regular singles' nights and there is a whole culture that surrounds it – especially where the gay scene is concerned. In the UK we may be a little more reserved about chatting to strangers while we shop, but it's an excellent way to strike up a conversation. What could be more normal than casually asking the glamorous woman standing next to you if she knows where the deli counter is? OK, it's not exactly a chat-up line, but it's a potential conversation opener, and who knows where it could lead? (With any luck, further than the deli counter!) You can always say, 'Sorry to bother you but. . .' before you ask a question, rather than sidling up to someone with your trolley, an expectant leer and a handful of German sausage! You may have your flirting tips and body language off pat, but you need to make sure the timing is right in order to put them into practice.

So therefore, the next time you think of sloping off to the supermarket in a pair of baggy running trousers, an old T-shirt and a pair of slippers, think again. You may be able to check out more than a week's groceries! Of course, just because someone is shopping alone, it doesn't necessarily mean they are single, but once you get into conversation with someone you can then establish how the land lies from there. Happy shopping!

DATING LOCATION: THE GYM

People types: Various – some ultra-fit, some just ultra hopeful but all with the same positive intention of looking and feeling better about themselves.

Forget about pubs and clubs, the number one venue for flirting is the gym. It's the perfect opportunity to look around you and see how everyone is exercising, chat to people about how a certain machine works or make remarks such as, 'Why do we do this to ourselves?' as we jog along the treadmill. Gyms are much less posey places than they used to be and the fact that the majority require membership immediately brackets members into a certain social circle where it's somehow 'safe' to talk to other people as they work out alongside you. 'A mixed steam room or sauna is probably best of all,' says Kieran Mullins, a personal trainer who has been given the nickname 'Dr Love' at the gym where he trains in north London. 'It's the easiest thing in the world to strike up a conversation in the sauna and now that gyms are becoming more like social clubs there are other places to flirt, like the juice bar or the newspaper area. I see it happening all the time and there's nothing subtle about it!'

As well as gym classes, many clubs also offer social evenings such as barbecues and picnics in the summer and parties in the winter. So if you've had your eye on someone but don't want to face them when you're spilling out of your cycling shorts, you can introduce yourself when you're looking a bit more glamorous. You've got any number of conversation openers available to you, such as, 'This makes a change from sweating it out on the treadmill,' to 'Do you train with Jason/Jane (add name as necessary)?' You can chat about how long you've both been going to the gym, whether you live nearby and so on, and before you know it, you could be more than just gym buddies.

A year's gym membership can cost around the same as one of the top dating agencies, so it's certainly not recommended if you seriously hate exercising or hate the idea of someone seeing you looking less than your best (full make-up is so not the thing to wear in a gym). However, if you think you may be into fitness, a gym is a great way of broadening your horizons, let alone making you feel better about yourself.

DATING LOCATION: SPORTING EVENTS AND ACTIVITIES

People types: Sports enthusiasts who are very focused on their hobby and use sporting interests as a release from their (often) very busy day jobs

If money doesn't run to a gym membership, but you are still into the idea of exercise along with the idea of meeting new people/potential dates, it's easy to find out what other sporting activities there are in your area. Whether it's supporting your local football team, going swimming (and having the odd chat between impressive laps up and down the pool) or trying something different like t'ai chi, it's easy enough to find out what's going on through your local paper or library. It's understandable that when you are stuck in a single rut it's hard to take the bull by the horns, but you have to make things happen. It's nerve-wracking at first, but you'll be amazed at how many people are in the same boat as you – and how non-threatening the whole thing is.

Although spectator events have the advantage of providing you with a subject that both you and a fellow spectator want to talk about, flirting is not the primary reason for being there. The downside is that social contact may be somewhat limited in terms of time, for example at a football match you're only really likely to meet new people at half time. The biggest exception to this rule is horseracing where the half-hour interval between each race is dedicated to being sociable. Racecourse etiquette means that strangers are actively encouraged to mix and according to research into social behaviour, because of the 'social microclimate' at race meetings, the racecourse is one of the best flirting environments in the UK.

The Intervarsity Club (IVC) network is the UK's original multi-activity club and while it doesn't call itself a singles' club, it's an excellent way to meet other single people and couples from all walks of life. Originally set up as a place for graduates to meet and mix, the IVC offers activities-orientated weekends (walking, watersports, biking and so on) plus fitness, cultural and social events around the UK. There are various local Intervarsity clubs around the UK with a combined total of 1,300 members between the ages of 25 and 45 (although there are no age limits to who can join). Some clubs offer open evenings in local hotels and clubs where you can go along, meet fellow members and find out about the club before deciding whether you'd like to join. So it's not as if you have to pay out a stash of cash before you can get a taste of what's involved. You don't need to be into sports, it's just a great social network and an easy way to make new friends. For more information, see the Resources section at the back of this book.

CASE STUDY

After her ten-year marriage broke down, 38-year-old Sarah, a teacher from York, joined the IVC and has never looked back.

I met someone quite quickly after my husband and I split up so it was only after that relationship ended that I found myself really feeling at a loose end. My best friend had also moved out of the area and so the two people that my social life revolved around suddenly weren't there any more. One evening I went to a house party with someone I knew who was a member of the IVC and met some of the other members there. They all seemed to have good jobs and great social lives because they were so involved in all the IVC activities, so I decided to join too. I liked the sound of the barbecues, wine-tastings, pub quizzes and dinners but I also play a lot of tennis so the sports aspect appealed too.

I joined in May 2001 and went to my first event on my own. As I'm a teacher I'm used to speaking to people I don't know and so I just went up to someone and said, 'Hi, I'm Sarah, how are you?' I find it very empowering to be able to get myself out and do something like that on my own. There are about a hundred members in the York group and two thirds are female and a third male, but I didn't join with the motive of meeting new men, it was just to make friends. I've now got a string of girlfriends from the IVC and we often go out on girls' nights out together. If we feel like clubbing and having a bit of a flirt it's a better idea to leave the male IVC members behind anyway! I'm really good friends with lots of them though and it's lovely to have male platonic friends for a change. We all go out in a mixed group and its lovely not to have heavy emotional ties with someone, just good friendships. And I've always got a party or a Sunday lunch or something to look forward to.

DATING LOCATION: EVENING CLASSES

People types: Ambitious mature students with spare time that they'd prefer to use on their mind, rather than their body (i.e. going to the gym or down the pub).

It sounds like an old chestnut, but evening classes are a tried and tested method of certainly meeting new people and even finding eligible single people. Just be careful which classes you pick. Teach Yourself Transcendental Meditation is obviously less likely to encourage you to interact with other class members than, say conversational Spanish, so pick your subjects with care. And for goodness sake, don't just do a blatantly male/female course just for the pick-up potential, people can see right through crass moves like that and quite honestly, you'll just look sad. Girls that go to car maintenance classes wearing 'cute' dungarees and don't know one end of a spanner from the other are just too ridiculous even to contemplate. So don't. As with any new social activity, use it as potential for meeting people generally – not just people of the opposite sex. Making new friends will help to broaden your horizons even further.

Learning places are great places to flirt because of shared student interests. The informal atmosphere and the fact that you have the same course in common immediately gives you a 'conversation window' and you won't need to struggle to think of things to talk about. Taking an evening course also opens up the possibility of extending the evening with a drink after class, therefore combining an even more relaxed atmosphere and a chance to talk about the evening's tuition (amongst other things). Oh yes, and you'll probably get to learn about other things into the bargain!

DATING LOCATION: SALSA NIGHTS

People types: Fun, outgoing, adventurous people who want to try something different.

For sure-fire one-to-one success, salsa! What could be better? Lively Spanish dancing, passionate music, sexy moves and fun, all wrapped up in lots of potential for single men and women to partner up. OK, there will be plenty of couples there and maybe the 'spare' females will outnumber the 'spare' men, but there is an increasing number of men who have cottoned on to the new craze. It's usually fairly cheap to have a go at salsa – from around £5 for a group session (to much more for individual lessons) or if it's in a Spanish bar, you are usually encouraged to buy drinks rather than pay an entrance fee. Music, dancing and alcohol make the environment even more conducive to romance and anyone can have a go at salsa. It's certainly a lot cooler than line-dancing, easier than ballroom dancing and more fun than both!

There are all sorts of other dancing courses available for those who feel so inclined – ballroom dancing has always had a massive following and there are almost endless other styles. But for beginners who may not want to take themselves too seriously and appreciate the added flirting opportunity, salsa will definitely help you make the right moves towards finding a date.

DATING LOCATION: CULTURAL CLUBS

People types: Those who get bored by 'just going to the pub', who aren't necessarily motivated by sports but like to let their vivid imaginations run wild.

Movie clubs are also becoming more popular and help take the emphasis of meeting other single people away from just pubs and bars. Instead, groups meet once a month to see a film, then have a drink/chat afterwards. Similarly, book clubs also happen up and down the country (usually once a month) bringing together disparate reading fans who take it in turns to choose a book and discuss it at the following meeting. The rest of the time is taken up with idle chit-chat, maybe a few drinks and if the social mix is right, maybe the odd bit of flirting. It's a good idea to research movie and book clubs fully as the type of people who join in can be very diverse, both in age range and cultural needs. They can be brilliant fun though, and even if you don't meet many potential dates, it's good to widen your social circles because it all adds up to more confidence – and fewer nights in feeling sorry for yourself.

The next chapter deals with groups which are specifically aimed at single people and are usually advertised in the personals sections of magazines and newspapers. Aside from these, you can also find plenty of other activities which may not be blatantly about potential romance opportunities but will certainly provide the right environment for it to happen.

Some of the large bookstore chains such as Waterstone's and Borders hold author talks, signings and poetry nights where you have the opportunity to meet people with similar literary interests to you. Signings tend to be held in the bookshops themselves, but author talks and poetry nights are held in places such as quieter bars and pubs where there is plenty of opportunity to interact. You've also got something obvious that you can talk about – favourite books, authors, poets – without having to go near the romance zone. If flirting happens, all well and good, if not, then you might meet a few nice friends along the way or you may simply have a good night out – and that can't be bad.

Ask about poetry nights, author talks and signings at bookshops in your local area or look at the Borders bookshop website: www.borders.co.uk or Waterstone's: www.waterstones.co.uk

DATING LOCATION: ON TV!

People types: Outgoing, confident, risk takers with nothing to lose.

For those with the confidence to put themselves in front of a TV camera – and not to mention millions of potential viewers – television dating shows are another option for single people. Since 1985 *Blind Date*, the UK's most famous and longest-running TV dating show has linked up over 900 couples, resulting in varying success. Meanwhile shows such as *Would Like To Meet*, *Perfect Match* and *ElimiDate* have also tried to play Cupid for total strangers. Not surprisingly, TV dating game shows receive an incredible amount of interest from would-be contestants and the criteria for each show and the selection processes vary considerably. Some hold regional auditions where contestants are asked to show off their party piece and encouraged to show the outgoing side of their personality through party games, while other shows find the contestants to fit a range of scenarios that they want to cover in a series. In the vast majority of cases, potential contestants can apply to be on a certain TV show via the channel's website or you can write to the show's producer c/o the TV channel.

Following the phenomenal success of television dating shows, the satellite TV station, The Dating Channel, links up more single people looking for love. The screen is divided into a message board with an interactive website – www.thedatingchannel.com – ad sites, and clips from single people (both straight and gay) who are looking to meet new people. You can text people that you see on TV and leave your own messages. So maybe it is possible to meet your soulmate while you're sitting at home watching TV.

DATING LOCATION: THE OFFICE

People types: Everyone from the boss to the geek in the IT department

Richard Reeves, author of *Happy Mondays: Putting the Pleasure Back into Work*, says that the workplace is the new dating agency. It's certainly true that many a relationship has blossomed around the vending machine. Figures from an Industrial Society report found that a third of people make most of their friends through work, and according to the employment consultancy Sanders and Sydney, a quarter of us meet our life partners at work. 'The last twenty years has seen the most dramatic rise in women returning to the workplace,' says Richard. 'This means that the workplace is much more mixed, so the opportunities for some kind of interaction have increased. Women are working alongside men in just as demanding roles, working longer hours and spending more time with their male colleagues. Not just because they are forced to, but because they want to.

'Also the nature of work has changed. The amount of time that we spend talking to colleagues has increased, and the fact that people often work together in an office environment physically encourages much closer working relationships. Therefore if a team of people is in a six-hour strategy meeting, there's bound to be some fantasising going on – if only to stay awake!'

An American study found that people are more likely to find relationships through work because the other ways that people traditionally used to meet has declined. The 'Faith, Space and Blood' theory – the idea that people meet because they share the same religion, home or extended network of family and friends – doesn't hold true anymore. The age-old dating mechanisms – marrying the boy next door, falling in love with someone from the same church or being introduced to your future wife by another family member – are on the decline. But when you see someone for forty hours a week and actually feel disappointed when it's time to go home at the end of the day, then Cupid is working overtime.

Some companies have a strict policy about dating in the workplace. As part of their employment contract, some companies make it a rule that colleagues cannot form romantic relationships. 'I think it's a ridiculous idea,' says Richard. 'I think they are kidding themselves thinking that it could ever work. If romance is forbidden it will have the opposite effect, drive it underground and make it even more enticing. In any case, research shows that the morale of the workers is much higher in workplaces where romance takes place.'

Each work environment has its own unwritten etiquette about flirting behaviour – who you can and can't flirt with, where to flirt and maybe when (lunch hour or near the end of the day). In some companies, flirting activity may centre around the coffee machine or smoking area, or maybe it will be restricted to after office hours in the nearby pub, where 'just the one' turns into a much more interesting working relationship. A word of warning though: make sure that you pick up the office etiquette about flirting from the most highly regarded members of staff, not the office clowns.

So the next time that someone from the office next door pops in to 'borrow' some teabags, make sure they make you a cup of tea too and maybe you can discuss what your plans are for after work. . .

CASE STUDY

Mia is a 29-year-old designer from South Africa who has certainly made the most of dating opportunities at work!

I work in publishing in a busy office of around forty people. I work closely with a team of about thirty of them and my first work romance was with a guy called Pete who was more into me than I was into him. It all started with flirty emails and then at the 2000 Christmas party he made his move. We were both quite drunk and had a good flirt and it all seemed like a good idea – until he kissed me. He had the biggest, sloppiest tongue and practically engulfed me. It was just awful. I made an excuse that the whole thing wasn't a good idea because of our work relationship and so on. Of course, if he had been a decent kisser I may have gone for it!

I was dating various other people that I met outside work but the hub of dating always seemed to be at the office, which brings us to Nat. He was tall, dark, handsome, intellectual, kind of scruffy and pretty much the opposite of what I'd usually go for physically. He was going through a nightmare of a romance and he used me as a sounding board and a bit of a shoulder to cry on. When he and his girlfriend finally split up we started seeing each other. We'd sneak off to the sixth floor for snogs and naughty stuff and he'd email me and suggest lunch at a pub where we knew the others wouldn't go. It was all totally secret. Neither of us wanted anyone to know, partly because he'd just split up with his girlfriend and partly because he was junior to me. I'd just been promoted and the whole thing seemed a bit weird. If we had decided it was going to be serious we would have made it public but it never seemed to get to that stage.

After about six months it was all getting a bit too hard. The sneaking off early from places to meet at each other's flats and the general secrecy of the whole thing seemed to be more trouble than it was worth. Then we all went away together on an office retreat. One night I got atrociously drunk and Nat went to bed in a strop. Now, me being the alcoholic I am, I decided to proposition this guy called Paul but he was in a steady relationship at the time so it was only ever going to be a flirt. However, another guy called James came on strong and I ended up going back to his room. After about an hour his phone rang and it was one of the other girls – saying she was feeling a bit lonely and would he like some company! The next day everything was totally cool and we both knew it was just a one-night stand. I made things up with Nat and continued to see him.

Then a new guy called Jon was taken on at work on a short-term contract and on his first day he made some wisecrack at me, then sent me an email to apologise. By this time I'd snogged three people, shagged two others and propositioned a sixth so I had no intention of letting this one go any further. Anyway, some time later we all went for a drink after work. I was still seeing Nat but that night he'd pissed me off about something and so I was feeling annoyed, unloved and a bit drunk. All this time Jon was throwing compliments at me and when we left the pub he just grabbed me and we had a snog. After that he said he wanted to escort me home and he jumped on to the tube with me and came all the way back to north London with me. By that stage I was thinking, 'This isn't really very funny,' and I really wanted to get rid of him. He insisted on walking me all the way home and said he wanted to come in and use the loo. I was getting really freaked out by him and I just wanted him to go. The following Sunday he turned up but I got my flatmate to say I was out. The next day at work he started emailing me constantly and then he turned up with a CD he'd made for me! How corny is that! Finally he gave me a written ultimatum which I just ignored.

Luckily soon after that he left and I decided that I wasn't going to date any more guys from work and Nat and I had kind of drifted apart. *Famous last words of course. A little while ago the guy who I'd propositioned at the retreat became single again and he asked me out. This one is going really well and he's lovely. I still don't know whether we're going to make it public though as it will be too complicated if it all falls apart. A couple of my girlfriends at work know about him but they're sworn to secrecy.*

It's been weird. All this has happened in the space of a year and a half – as well as all of the other dates that I've had along the way. I do feel a bit of a slag, but I've had so much fun! I don't know why the majority of people I seem to date all come from work; I guess it's because I'm lazy. I've run out of eligible guys at my place though – I'm thinking of swapping with my flatmate now and giving her workmates a go!

DATING DATA – POINTS TO REMEMBER
WIDENING YOUR SOCIAL CIRCLES

→ Start making conscious moves to expand your social life and research into social opportunities in your local area.
→ Find out about clubs that involve your hobby or look into evening courses.
→ Consider joining a social activity group such as the IVC.
→ If you go to a gym, ask if they have a list of social events for members.
→ Make use of flirting opportunities at work.

7 DATING – THE OPTIONS AND THE LINGO

The difference between small ads, dating agencies, Internet dating, speed dating and other dating opportunities. How much they all cost and how to read between the lines.

So, you've learned the lingo, found your confidence and feel ready to hit the dating scene. It's one thing to have signed up for evening classes, joined a gym and used every flirting environment and opportunity possible. But if you are still finding it hard to find a date, maybe you should think about taking the bull by the horns and go straight to where dates are (almost) guaranteed. Whether it's perusing the lonely hearts columns, joining a dating agency, going on a singles' holiday or logging on to an Internet dating site, it's no-nonsense 'I'm looking for a mate' territory and cuts to the chase of your motives for wanting to get to know someone better.

Many people see these contrived methods of introduction as a bit of a last resort – the last chance saloon for people who have failed to meet someone in the 'usual' way – whatever that is. No matter how right-on people say they are about it, there's still something of a stigma attached to using dating agencies, small ads and so on. Slowly but surely, however, people are wising up to the benefits, as Karen Mooney from agency Sarah Eden Introductions explains: 'The stigma is certainly not as bad as it used to be and definitely not so apparent for the under-35s. In the same way that if people want to find a house they go to an estate agency, and if they want a job they'll go to an employment agency, if they want a date they can use an introduction agency. It's that simple. It's usually people who don't know much about agencies that think they are just for people with social inadequacies. It's only when you come into an agency or use a singles service that you see that people are completely 'normal' busy professionals – just like yourself, and there's nothing weird or sad and lonely about it. People are very misinformed about the whole subject and they could be missing out on the chance of real future happiness.'

American sociologist Pepper Schwartz, who is the author of several books on relationships, says that there is still a stigma attached to using a dating agency because being lonely is such a hard thing to admit. 'We're all supposed to be so devastatingly attractive that things come our way, and the fact that we have to advertise ourselves isn't seen to be romantic. We're not supposed to be seen as needy, and advertising to some people is seen as crass, but now there are cultural shifts. Because dating agencies and lonely hearts dating is such a common thing now it is becoming more commonplace. It's like the waterfall analogy – if enough water falls into the trough, it will eventually fill up and spill over. And in the same way with dating agencies, if there's enough usage, validation and practice, dating agencies will spill over into different parts of society.'

Pepper says that because people are getting together so much later in life there isn't the pool of 'eligible' single people that there was when we were at school and at college. 'Suddenly you're 35 and single again and where can you meet someone? The fact that so many people have met other people who are totally socially acceptable through lonely hearts means they can't be seen as a last resort any more. It's just the fact that 'conventional' meeting places such as dinner parties/parties or meeting other people through friends is a much lower risk than dating outside your social circle.' The idea of meeting a total stranger who is totally unrelated to your social group can be a real leap into the unknown. It's human nature to be adverse to change. But those who have found partners this way or just widened their social circles as a result of joining a dating agency, will confirm how successful, entertaining, confidence-building and anecdote-inducing they can be.

DATING AGENCIES

Considered to be the most committed method of introduction, there are countless dating agencies all over the world boasting an almost 100 per cent success rate in terms of compatibility and being able to match up individuals. The UK's largest agency, Dateline, uses computer matching but many smaller agencies hand-pick mates for dates and do the matchmaking on a one-to-one basis. Chapter

9 deals with dating agencies in more detail and the costs involved – which can vary considerably.

SMALL ADS

Almost any magazine or newspaper with classified advertising pages will have some kind of 'personal' section – either a lonely hearts listing or advertisements for introduction agencies. Traditionally with lonely hearts columns, you either place your own advertisement or respond to someone else's ad by post, and letters are forwarded to the relevant box number. Nowadays, however, it's more common to see a telephone-based service. This allows you to place an ad for free by calling a number and leaving a message and then collect any messages that have been recorded for you by people who have seen your ad in the magazine/newspaper. When the person who is advertising calls to leave their voice message, they are also given the option to create the advertisement which will appear in print, or have the print ad created for them based on the details they leave in their message. The publication then prints your advertisement about a week later (depending on the frequency of the mag/paper) with a phone number allocated for each entry. Interested readers can then call up the voice mailbox, listen to the recorded message and decide whether or not to leave their details. Then it's up to the person who has advertised to decide whether to respond. In the grand scheme of things it's a relatively cheap way of meeting people as calls can cost as little as £1, but in reality you are likely to clock up more of a bill as calling small ads can become very addictive! Just one more, then just one more and suddenly you have a serious phone bill.

CASE STUDY

Jez, 34, from London advertises himself in the lonely hearts pages to broaden his social circle – and increase his potential for romance.

I have been putting an advertisement in the Guardian newspaper's Soul Mates section for the last three years. I do it every summer because I like to get out and meet women – in the winter I'm quite happy hibernating and just staying at home watching television on my own. I've been single for about four years now and because I live in London I find it very hard to meet people. My friends all seem to be married and are more into putting shelves up and having babies than having fun, so Soul Mates works really well for me. I do it primarily to meet new people and have some fun – not really to have any kind of serious relationship. In fact I think it's difficult to have a 'normal' relationship with people you meet this way because it's quite artificially set up. Saying that though, I did go out with someone for a year and a half who I met through one of my previous ads.

I usually say that I'm doing this to expand my social circles and that I look like 'a gay football hooligan' – I've got a bald head and poncey glasses. I'm 34, I've got a good sense of humour (GSOH) and I'm looking for an intelligent female with a killer sense of humour for 'friendship first' (FF) and anything that comes after that is a bonus! The first time I put my ad in I said I've been described as cute and handsome and I got 78 replies! One time I said that I worked in pornography and was a part-time male stripper and I only got eight replies and another time I got 34 replies which was about right I suppose.

I start by listening to all of the recorded messages and giving everyone marks out of ten. It sounds a bit brutal but it's very difficult to evaluate them otherwise. I listen to what they have to say, the way that they say it, whether or not they have picked up on anything I've said and the description that they give of themselves. If they say they are attractive they instantly get extra bonus points – even if they are not really! I want to meet people who have got lots to say for themselves and I'd much rather meet someone who is interesting than someone who has a high-powered job. I can also tell if someone is desperate or nervous by the message they leave because they have a kind of overbearing, pleading, tone!

I try and make contact with as many people as I can. If someone leaves their mobile number I usually drop them a text message and ask them if they have an email address where I can write to them. I think that's a much more relaxed way of getting to know someone than just ringing them up out of the blue. That way I can send them a picture of what I look like so that I won't be a crashing disappointment to them if we meet!

After a bit of to-ing and fro-ing with emails and conversations I'll suggest we meet for a drink and go on from there. I've had loads of dates this way and so I'm not particularly nervous about it, although I have regretted certain dates where I've let things go too far and felt really bad about it afterwards. Blokes do have a conscience too although I've discovered that there are plenty of girls who are only in it for the sex! My worst date was with a woman who turned up with two kids in the back of her car. She couldn't get a babysitter and it was too late to cancel, so she brought them along! Twenty minutes later I was sitting watching Byker Grove with a plate of fish fingers and chips on my lap!

I was terrified about my mates finding out that I did this kind of dating but when my flatmate put two and two together and I told everyone my mates thought it was the most heroic thing they had ever heard of and were really envious. There's still a part of me that thinks the whole thing is totally artificial though – the fact that people can't find partners through 'normal' ways. But I look at it as just a way to make new friends. When you 'click' with someone it's fantastic and I've met people who I really think will be friends for life. But I hate the idea of being some kind of Chinese plate spinner – keeping several dates going without being totally straight with them all. Therefore I try and stagger dates and let them run their course. At the end of my recorded message I always say 'thanks for listening and I hope you get what you're looking for' and that's what it's all about at the end of the day.

CASE STUDY

Torn between buying a designer coat or joining a dating agency, thirty-year-old Natalie decided on the former.

Having split up with my husband of six years, which was very unpleasant, I moved to a new area in north London and it was a huge adjustment. I really wanted to meet some new people and so I thought of joining one of the bigger dating agencies. I booked an appointment and the rep was going to come around and see me one Saturday lunchtime, so I thought I'd do some shopping beforehand. I saw an amazing Dolce and Gabanna coat in a shop window and I just had to try it on. It was £450 which was about the price of membership to the dating agency and after a lot of agonising I decided I needed the coat more than a dating agency. So I rang them up with a spurious excuse and thought that was that.

A few weeks later I was flicking through the Guardian newspaper and thought I'd call up a couple of the Talking Hearts (recorded small ads). I soon realised that it would be a lot cheaper to record my own message than to listen to loads of other people so I spent an entire evening recording my own, going over and over it again and again until I was happy with how it sounded. I described my colouring, my height and my job (I'm a social worker) and just waffled on about all sorts of stuff, but after a while I got a bit frustrated and just hung up – not thinking that the ad would actually be processed. But then a few days later I got confirmation in the post that an ad would be running the following week.

I'd forgotten I'd done the ad but one Saturday night my friend came over and we listened to the replies – there were seventy of them! Which on its own was absolutely lovely and an incredible ego boost. They all seemed like really nice normal people (apart from one guy who suggested a threesome!). So then my friend and I took it in turns to listen to the replies and gave them a star rating – one was OK, two was good, three was excellent. At one point she started waving her arms around and said I just had to hear one of 'hers'. It was from a guy called Paul, a radio producer who loved reading (and hated Jeffrey Archer, which made me laugh) and sounded really nice. A couple of days later I took the bull by the horns and called him and he was lovely – and he only lived about ten minutes from where I lived.

We arranged to meet and I got the shock of my life when a man fitting his description (5 foot 7 and mixed race) turned up brandishing a magnum of champagne and about forty roses. I deliberately hadn't made any effort with the way I looked because I didn't want to build the date up into something bigger than it was. I'd chewed off all of my lipstick and looked a bit bedraggled and was generally feeling quite negative about it. Anyway, just then the 'real' Paul appeared and we started chatting as if we'd known each other for years. I didn't immediately fancy him but we got on so well that by the next time we saw each other I'd started to change my ideas a bit. I was determined I wasn't going to let him get away!

On our second date he lost his keys and he came back to my place which was a bit awkward as neither of us wanted anything to happen. He was really sweet and said, 'I really like you, but. . .' at which point I thought he was going to finish with me. However the end of the sentence was, 'I'd like to take things really slowly,' and I was so relieved.

Things actually moved pretty fast after that. We started talking about marriage about three months into our relationship and got engaged officially on my birthday in February 2001. We were married in June 2002 and it's just been wonderful.

My advice to anyone is not to make any kind of assumptions about lonely hearts or dating agencies. My friends were all really freaked that I met Paul that way but nobody needs to know that that's how you met someone. It's all completely anonymous anyway and if you decide that you don't want to meet anyone you don't have to return any of the calls. But all I can say is, 'Go for it!' I'm so glad that I did!

SINGLES' NIGHTS

Black-tie balls, dinner parties, discos, sporting events, group theatre trips. . . Check out any personals columns and you'll see advertisements for a range of cultural events which take the 'are you single?' and other testing-the-water questions out of the equation. Singles' social clubs tend to attract thirty-somethings upwards and aim to attract busy professionals who want to widen their social circles – not just find potential dates.

Dinner Dates now has 14,000 members and is the original social events agency in the UK. It was set up in 1989 by Hilly Marshall who stresses that Dinner Dates is not a dating agency per se but says, 'Dating is a numbers game and the more people that you meet, the more chance that you have of meeting someone who is right for you.' It costs £150 plus VAT to join Dinner Dates and then it's up to you to plan your social calendar. You can choose to join in black tie and other special dinner parties at various five-star locations where the maximum number is 32, or perhaps go to one of their buffets for sixty. There are also various cultural packages including trips to the Tate Modern gallery plus dinner, dinner and a night at the opera and outdoor events such as polo matches, Henley Regatta and Ascot. Every month a holiday is organised and there are eight members' balls a year for three hundred people. Of course, all events are extra to the £150 membership but the majority of social agencies work in a similar way.

Smaller agencies such as Across the Room have a tighter catchment area, both geographically and in age group. Eleanor De Goni-Parkes set up her agency in 1998 in order to bring together single people in their thirties, forties and fifties in the Essex, Hertfordshire, Kent and Suffolk area. £125* buys you lifetime membership and a list of all of the weekly events; you then have to pay from £15 for a party night buffet and disco to £40 for a black-tie gala dinner.

Similar clubs offer other kinds of 'relaxing social evenings for professional single people'. Billed not so much as a matchmaking opportunity but a friendly club, the AL Arts Club in London costs £120 for a year's membership. Members meet once a month at an exclusive art gallery in north London where they have drinks then go on to a variety of concerts, arts and theatrical events. Patricia Bellotti who set up the club in 2001 with her business partner Janice says the club works on different levels for different people. 'All of our members are in the thirty to fifty age group and have joined for a mixture of reasons. Some have very busy careers and don't have the time to organise their social lives, others are divorced and want to meet a new circle of friends, and some just want to meet other people with the same interest in the arts. The atmosphere is very different to a singles' night because we always hold our evenings in our own art gallery, which is a great venue to meet up. There are always exhibitions being shown so it doesn't feel strange at all – there's no pressure and people don't feel they are being eyed up or pushed together. Inevitably people are getting together as they share the same interests but it's happening in a very relaxed way.'

Further south, Eligible Balls are singles' parties that are held in Brighton around every month. Guests are encouraged to interact with each other by playing 'low-key' games such as 'nuts and bolts' where the men are given nuts and the women are given bolts and they have to find their partner. 'It's a great way to get people talking to each other and it's really just a bit of fun,' says party organiser Nigel Berman. 'We get around 50 to 100 coming to the parties which we hold in all sorts of interesting venues around the city. And because of the beach and the number of hotels, we get people from all over the place coming down to the balls.' It's just £20 a ticket, which includes a free drink – and maybe either a nut or a bolt – so, as Nigel says, 'It's a great way for stylish, interesting and creative people aged 25-plus to meet.'

Some of the bigger dating agencies also lay on social evenings as part of the membership package, so it's worth shopping around if this is an area of particular interest to you.*

CASE STUDY

Fate and a pre-organised dinner date brought 39-year-old Roy and 41-year-old Serena together.

Roy: *I can't stand discos and crowds and I find it difficult to meet people with the same cultural interests as me so that's why I joined Dinner Dates. I read about it in the Sunday Times and sent off for the brochure. I'd been a member of an executive dating agency but it was expensive and a disaster but I liked the sound of Dinner Dates. The first date I went on was at the Roof Garden Terrace in London and it was excellent. Around eight of us met up and it was really enjoyable. I was very nervous about walking into the room on my own but everyone was very relaxed and familiar and it didn't seem strange at all when we were all introduced. We all got on really well and we have stayed in touch, even though there was no romance on that occasion. It was just great to meet intelligent people who had something to talk about and who I felt I had something in common with.*

Although the idea of dating was in the background I enjoyed going to Dinner Dates just for the social events. People seem to discuss more in groups and I met some great people and had a few dates but nothing of an enduring nature. Then there was a Hallowe'en party and I bumped into Serena. Normally we would

* For more details about all of the social events agencies listed see the Resources section at the back of this book

never have met as you are always positioned in age groups – men are always seated with younger women – so maybe it was fate that we met.

Serena: *It was my first Dinner Dates event so I was very nervous and I remember seeing Roy because he was wearing a striped blazer. I went to the bar to get a drink and we just started chatting and I thought he was really nice.*

Roy: *We hardly spoke after that because of the seating arrangements but we just clicked when we started talking to each other and I really took a shine to her. I spoke to someone at the agency the next day and said that I'd met someone but that I doubted if she would remember me, but she did and she also agreed to meet up so we went on a date together. We went to see a show and then went out for a meal afterwards and got on really well. We both felt really comfortable and relaxed together.*

After that we started seeing more of each other and on midsummer's day 2002 I proposed to her and she accepted. We plan to get married at a ski resort with just close friends and family and have a big party when we get home.

I've told the majority of friends how we met but Serena is a little more private about it. I don't really see any stigma attached to joining something like Dinner Dates. The only stigma is what's inside you and how you feel about it. People should understand that there's no longer the structure and the events that there used to be for single people, there's just this idiocy that you're supposed to meet people by accident in a darkened room with music blaring out in the background.

Serena: *Neither of us was remotely inexperienced about relationships and we both had had short-term incompatible relationships but I just loathed the idea of being chatted up in a bar.*

Roy: *I've recommended Dinner Dates to several of my friends and my brother and we both still attend events, but on the 'staff' table so that we don't mislead any of the members. It doesn't feel remotely odd though and it's so refreshing to meet similar people in such pleasant circumstances. I'd definitely recommend it to anyone.*

SPEED DATING

It has been calculated that it takes between ninety seconds and four minutes to decide if we fancy someone, which could explain the new craze in speed dating. You no longer have to sit through a dreadful date for hours with someone who you know that you don't click with or endure a terrible blind date with someone with as much sex appeal as a squashed vole. Deborah Sherbourne runs 40datesAnight with her partner Marcel Knobil, an evening where eighty unattached professionals (forty men, forty women) meet up for champagne and canapés in a central London bar and each person has three minutes to talk to each other before moving on to the next 'date'. 'We give each person a form to fill in and as each chat is concluded, you can tick off whether you'd be interested in seeing that person again, leave it blank or just write an 'f' if you'd like to stay in touch as friends. At the end of the day we compare all of the forms and where there are matching ticks, we forward on their email details 48 hours later. It's pay-as-you-go dating, pure and simple.' To attend one of the parties costs £40 and the majority of people are between 28 and 41, and more parties are being planned for the future. There are many similar agencies offering speed-dating nights, for example Gorgeous Networks. They operate in a similar way in that you only have a short amount of time to get to know someone and then move on and they are proving incredibly successful. They cut to the chase of what dating is all about if your number one priority is physical attraction. The really clever thing is to use the time wisely or you may miss out on an opportunity or fail to see your soulmate lurking behind those cheesy chat-up lines.

CASE STUDY

Forty-year-old recruitment consultant James from Chester took the plunge and tried speed dating and has never looked back.

I'd been married for nine years and in March 2002 my wife and I decided it just wasn't working and called it a day. When you're in a married crowd, people are very comforting and supportive of each other, but you don't tend to meet any single people unless they are friends who are also divorced or separated. I read an article about speed dating in the States and I thought it was a brilliant idea to meet people – not just single women but also single men that you could meet up with who weren't just other divorcees. I went along to 40datesAnight in May and was very impressed at how organised the set up was. It was like being in a bar with forty available women – and you can chat up all of them! Normally you could be in a bar and spend forty minutes chatting someone up and not get anywhere because you find out they weren't available anyway, but doing 40datesAnight was great, it was an awesome experience. With some people you just click immediately and with others you have absolutely no chemistry, but it's not a big deal because you just move on. I wasn't looking for the love of my life, just someone who I could go out for dates with – maybe go out for a meal, have drinks with or just a cuddle.

Speed dating gives you a real opportunity to be totally spontaneous and in three minutes you can find out an awful lot about a person. When people asked about me I told them that I'd just come out of a marriage, was seriously damaged goods, that I couldn't commit to anything further than the next twelve hours and that I'm a complete nightmare, but it didn't seem to put people off. At the end of the session there were 25 people who I was interested in seeing again and out of those I had seventeen women who were interested in me. I had three proper dates after that and I have met other single women through some of the others, which is another great way that speed dating widens your social circles. My shrink told me that I had to get out there and meet people, and now I have about three dates a week with different people. My philosophy in life is that I was rejected by my wife after ten years so if I'm rejected by someone who I meet in a bar or at a singles party like 40datesAnight it won't be the end of the world.

SINGLES' HOLIDAYS

Holiday brochures are chock full of smiling couples and happy families and many singletons dread the whole idea of going on holiday. And if you can't pair up with a fellow singleton and feel cheesed off if you have to pay a single-person supplement, the options can be quite limited. As Chapter 5 describes, one way to broaden your social circles is to do a course and this is a great way of getting a holiday into the bargain. italiancookerycourse.com is just one residential course which actually bills itself as a singles' holiday where up to fourteen students meet in a friendly and informal environment, learn to cook and get to savour the delights afterwards. Much more civilised and subtle then a hit-and-miss blind date.

Solos Holidays, the market leader in singles' holidays, offers eight hundred holidays a year in over seventy countries. All prices are based on single rooms and all holidays are escorted by a tour manager who acts as a social manager to the group, organising group activities and get-togethers. However, Solos' spokesperson Kirstin Monk insists it's not a dating agency. 'We're a holiday company for unattached, divorced, widowed or newly single people aged 25 to 69. The idea behind the company isn't to find a mate but to offer the security to people of travelling together and knowing they are with like-minded individuals in the same age group.' Holidays are organised in age groups of 25–45, 28–55 and 45–69 with a 50/50 male–female ratio and with some holidays (such as golfing breaks) open to all age groups. 'It's a one-stop shop for singles' holidays,' says Kirstin.

Other companies, such as singles-holidays.demon.co.uk offer holiday encounters ideally suited to men and women over 35 from a fortnight in the Gambia to New Year in Norwich for small groups of between twelve and twenty. Other holiday companies offering packages specifically for singles are: solitairhols.co.uk, trekamerica.com, encounter.co.uk, travel-quest.co.uk (see Resources section at the back of the book).

CASE STUDY

Singles' holidays may not be for everyone, but if you've got the nerve to book one, you're halfway there, says 36-year-old David, a marketing manager from Plymouth.

I went on my first singles' holiday in 2000. I go on holiday a few times a year and so that limits my choice of people to go with as my single friends only tend to go away once a year and I can't always go away with couples and just be a 'spare man'. Also, other people's travel dates don't always coincide with when I can get time off. That's why I started looking into singles' holidays but once I'd decided, I found it hard to find holiday companies who specifically offer them. There were things like Club 18–30 of course but I didn't want to go with a company where there would be big groups of lads or couples, I wanted a holiday with lots of other individuals. When I booked with Sovereign Small World Holidays I checked with the operator that there would be lots of thirty-something women there and I booked a week in the sun in the Costa Del Sol. It was £650 for an all-inclusive 3–4 star villa in the middle of nowhere and the couple that owned the place did all the cooking and we had barbecues every night. It was lovely.

There were fifteen of us on the trip, some in their late twenties, some thirties, forties and even fifties, but mainly thirty-something girls which was fine by me! Most people were really friendly but although everyone had had the guts to go on a singles' holiday, some people just didn't have the confidence to mix. It was a good range of people though – everyone from waitresses and mechanics through to management consultants and people who worked in the City. I got on really well with people there and after about four days I had got it together with a girl called Jessica who was divorced with three children and lived in Somerset.

It was the first holiday romance I'd ever had and we got on really well, but when we met up again in England the spark wasn't there. In the cold light of day, the difficulties of seeing a divorced mother of three who lives in a different part of the country are a million miles away from child-free, hassle-free barbecues in Spain.

I went on my second singles' holiday a year later and this time I stayed at a hotel south of Seville and there were 25 of us. I didn't enjoy this holiday quite so much as the first one as I found a lot of the women wanted to rely on the hotel for entertainment and wouldn't try any of the local bars or restaurants. I made a good group of friends though and I've stayed in touch with one of the guys from there, but there was no romance with any of the women this time. I wasn't worried though. For me, going on a singles' holiday was about enjoying myself with other single people rather than being surrounded by couples. As long as you're in a big enough group you can strike a chord with a couple of people and

*it's good to meet other single men in the same position. I'd
definitely recommend that single people really think about going
on a singles' holiday. It is a bit daunting at first, but once you've
booked the holiday the hard bit's over. All you have to do is enjoy
yourself.*

INTERNET DATING

Current statistics suggest that in less than three years' time, over
50 per cent of single people will meet a partner online. In the
United States, Internet dating is so successful that it is called
'hyperdating' or 'man shopping' (it works equally well if you happen
to be 'woman shopping'). People set up dates online – sometimes
several in one night and then spend an evening on the net. Just
imagine – you don't even need to get changed out of your pyjamas,
brush your hair or finish eating a plate of fish and chips before you
log on and start your romantic date.

According to research at Bath University, a third of all net users try
out the web to find a relationship, but as Internet dating is so often
confused with the unregulated world of chat-rooms, it has been
subject to really bad press. The opportunities for misuse and the
exploitation of minors have lead to the idea that any kind of
personal introduction via the Net is intrinsically dodgy. 'The whole
idea of Internet dating has been tarnished because of chat-rooms,'
says Andy McCabe, who set up the Internet dating agency
www.loveandfriends.com. 'Chat-rooms are the lowest level of
electronic introduction. They're unregulated and a complete free-
for-all – anyone can go into a chat-room and there's no investment
in terms of money or personal time.'

With Internet dating you have to spend time making up a personal
profile of yourself and being thoughtful about the whole process.
The fact that you have to pay any money at all up front means that
you are less likely to abuse the system. 'It's only £10 to sign up to
loveandfriends.com, but people won't even pay that if they are only
out for instant kicks,' says Andy.

Internet dating has been up and running on an informal basis since
the Internet began. In the early 90s it was in its embryonic stage
and had restricted access to people who were mostly either

academics or computer geeks. But as computers have become more mass market and more people have access to a PC, so the target market has broadened and now there are Internet agencies for all ages. There's www.wejustclicked.com, www.woowho.com, www.onesaturday.com, www.oneandonly.com, www.datingdeluxe.com, www.pearmatch.co.uk, and so the list goes on. (See Resources section at the back of the book.) In 1998 www.udate.com became the tenth largest Internet dating site in the world and on Valentine's Day 2001 it merged with another site and now boasts over ten million members.

'When it comes to the Internet, people always like to boast big numbers of users,' says Toby Jones, who set up www.WheresMyDate.com in 1999. 'But it's more important to find out how many active members an agency has to see how successful it is going to be for you. The people who use WheresMyDate are all active members with the majority of people logging on in their lunch hours at work or from 5 p.m. onwards.' Rather than being sad computer geeks with too much time on their hands, they're time-poor and use the Internet to fit dating around their busy lives.

HOW DOES IT ALL WORK?

Have a surf around some of the Internet dating agencies on offer (see the Resources section at the back of the book for a selection of addresses). Some agencies, such as loveandfriends.com and wheresmydate.com offer a mainly free service and you can access the site straight away. You can view members' profiles, check out their photographs and their general personal details, then scroll down to read about the next person and so on. In the case of loveandfriends.com, you can send quick emails for free, but if you want to find out more specific information about a person (say for instance you want to meet someone who's into dancing or a *Guardian* reader) you have to pay for the service of having a more accurate selection. You can also pay to send smileys, winks and greetings to other members. loveandfriends.com have ten thousand members and claim to offer the most comprehensive questionnaire in terms of personal details in order to be able to match people more fully. Andy explains the thinking behind it all:

'We call loveandfriends.com "Internet Dating for Thinking People" and in what has become a very huge marketplace it offers a service for intelligent like-minded individuals.'

wheresmydate.com offers a free week's membership to entice people to try Internet dating. Once you log on, as on other dating sites you are asked to fill in a few details such as:

→ **I am a woman/man (delete as applicable).**
→ **Looking for a woman/man (delete as applicable).**
→ **Between the ages of (choose age range).**
→ **In. . . (choose area).**

And so on. . .

You are then quickly matched with people who fit your criteria and in the case of wheresmydate.com you can then access their 'Can Openers.' These are information categories that are unique to the site that aim to bring out more of each member's personality, as Toby Jones explains. 'For example, we ask questions like, "What are your three favourite films and why? If you had £10,000, how would you spend it? And, If you could invite any six people to a dinner party (living or dead) who would they be and why?" It brings out the personality in our members and means that people go on more than face value.' However, face value is important says Toby. 'Our members generally get eight times more response if they upload a photo with their description.'

The reason that Internet dating has caught on so massively is because people can be totally in control of the whole dating scenario. You can log on at your leisure and make all of the moves in your own time – even in the middle of the night if you fancy a midnight flirt. Even the most shy person in the world can drop someone an email to say hi and check out the details of anyone who has sent an email to them. 'I think it's always nice if people can acknowledge emails so that people don't feel snubbed,' says Toby, 'but the important thing is to use Internet dating as your own agency. Send out lots of messages – you know how nice it is to hear the "ping" of an email – and just enjoy yourself. You've got absolutely nothing to lose!'

You can flirt to your heart's content without anyone seeing you blush and spend time phrasing and answering questions that would normally leave you tongue-tied. Trish McDermot, who is Vice

President of Romance at <u>match.com</u>, the world's biggest Internet dating agency, says, 'The most successful online daters seem to be the ones who don't get their hopes up too much and go on as many dates as their salary allows. Dating is a numbers game.'

TEXT DATING

A step on from Internet dating is text dating. This is a service that links up members of various agencies via text messages. <u>www.twoscompany.co.uk</u> has introduced a messaging service that not only informs existing members of new members who fit their criteria, but also tells you when you have new messages from other members.

Taking texting even further, one of the most innovative forms of singles' nights comes courtesy of a company called textravagent. Here, single people are whisked away on a mystery evening of dating and socialising in London. Armed with your mobile phone, you decipher text messages that are sent to you, guiding you to two bars and a final 'after party' for 150 single people. Like other dating services, the member signs up and sends in a personal profile that is then matched up with other compatible singles. Once the Cupids have done their work, the couples are then issued with a series of instructions of how to meet and identify each other. Couples meet up in pairs of two – to get to know other 'textravagent' party-goers and then everyone convenes for a huge party of newly matched couples.

For more information, see the Resources section at the back of the book.

ASTRAL DATING

Astral dating is a method of romantically analysing and matching up compatible birth charts. Like Internet dating, there are scores of astral dating agencies in the United States, but it is a relatively new concept in the UK. WheresMyDate.com has introduced astral dating to its package of Internet services, using professional astrologers to match up birth charts for more compatibility than just age, location and interests. Any of the bigger search engines will also direct you to astral dating agencies such as Astral Connections (www.astralconnections.com) who promise to match people who can 'generate a compatible and harmonious environment when put together'. If you are a firm believer that your fate is written in the stars, this could be the perfect dating method for you. By checking 'astral energy make-up' and how 'astral energies combine', astral matchmakers can deduce whether it is a 'positive or negative combination'. Like many such dating services, registration is free and charges comes into play when the user wants to obtain more information or links with potential astral partners.

SAFETY FIRST

A word of warning though, with any kind of dating, if you do decide to get in contact with someone, keep your details brief and private. There are a lot of strange people out there – even if they do have nice, non-psycho-looking photographs that are instantly available to the whole of cyberspace. Don't give out your home telephone number or your address, and if you decide to meet up with someone in person, make sure you follow the dos and don'ts of dating (see Chapter 10). At the end of the day, if you've followed all of the rules and it still doesn't work for you, you can always compare notes on www.wildxangel.com which is a website dedicated entirely to Internet dating disasters. There really is, quite literally, something for everyone.

CASE STUDY

Helen, 32, is a proofreader from Hertfordshire. She always hated the idea of joining a dating agency and was fed up with never meeting anyone new.

I decided to give Internet dating a go after someone I work with suggested I had a look at the loveandfriends.com website. I suppose I had preconceptions about the kind of people that would do Internet dating – that they'd all be sad and lonely desperate loser types who can't get dates the normal way. But why should they be? I mean, I'm a beautiful young lady and I can't get dates the so called 'normal' way so why should I be any different either? The trouble is that you tend to stick with the same circles of people and always do the same 'safe' things and it just seems a hassle to try and go out and meet people. It's a case of been there, done that.

Anyway, I had a look at the quick search options and at first glance I saw men with common interests to me. They all seemed educated, read the same newspapers as me and listed the same kind of books that I read and films that I like, so I was really pleasantly surprised. After I'd thought about it for a while I decided to log in my own details and I emailed three of the people, saying, 'Hi, I'm Helen, I liked what you had to say about so and so. . .' I wasn't nervous at all about doing it, because it didn't feel real in a way. I was just excited about what would happen next. It was just like a game, a bit of fun.

That day I had about seven emails back which was incredible! I was really chuffed and after that I just became addicted to it! I thought, 'Oh, no, I'll never have a life now – I'll just spend all my free time on the Internet!' My friend came over that weekend and she got really into it too! We ended up fighting over who we were going to send emails to!

After a few days I narrowed my email relationships down to about three or four people. One of them, Mark, sounded really nice. Neither of us had a picture of ourselves on the site at that stage and he said, 'Let's get this thing over with!' and so we both uploaded pictures. I looked really serious in mine and I got a bit nervous that I'd never hear from him again, but I heard back from him straight away. After that things got a bit more flirty – it's almost as if you're not 'real' until you put a picture of yourself out there. Then he took the plunge and said, 'Here's my number, call me,' which I did. I was incredibly nervous but he sounded really mellow and easy to talk to and we decided to make a date and meet up.

I was almost sick with nerves on the night that we met. I walked into the pub where we'd arranged to meet and saw someone looking at me. I didn't recognise him because he had come straight from work and was wearing a suit, so I just walked straight out of the other door. He followed me out and shouted, 'Helen!' then gave me a really big hug and a kiss on the cheek, which was lovely and immediately put me at ease. We talked and talked and talked and drank and drank and he kept hugging me. Then one of the hugs turned into a snog and it was just lovely!!! We were like teenagers snogging in the corner of a pub but it was just so nice.

My friends were in the area (I'd told them where I was going to be) and I got a lift home with them and Mark emailed me at around lunchtime the next day saying how much he'd enjoyed our date. Because we'd sent so many emails to each other we'd found out quite a lot about each other and so the whole thing seemed really easy. It wasn't contrived like some of the other blind dates I've been on.

We arranged to meet up again and on our next date he came over to my place for lunch. As soon as he walked through the door we practically pounced on each other but managed to restrain ourselves – at least until after lunch! The next day I went to a wedding in Switzerland and when I got back he was waiting on my doorstep!

It all seemed a bit too good to be true and the very next day I had a feeling that something wasn't quite right but I couldn't put my finger on what it was. We made a date to meet up the following weekend but he emailed me the day before and said he wanted to call it a day. The weird thing was he didn't know why he wanted to end it either, it just didn't feel right. So that was that. It was over as quickly as it had started.

The experience didn't put me off at all though. I quickly contacted one of the others who I'd met through the website and we met up and had a fantastic date! Now I think I've got some sort of dating bug – I don't know whether I'll ever want to stick with just one person because it's so much fun, and such an ego boost knowing that there are so many single men out there.

The best thing about the whole experience for me is discovering that you can get to know someone from the inside out, rather than the outside in. So much of attraction these days is based on face value and whether you instantly fancy someone, but the way I've met up with my recent dates is totally different – based on shared interests and how their minds work. Recently I got an email from someone who saw my details on the site and is setting up a book club for some of the members and he asked me if I want to go along, which I *definitely will do. In the last six weeks I've had more fun than I've had in years and it's all down to playing on the Internet. Brilliant.*

BE PREPARED FOR NEGATIVE FEEDBACK

For every person who is completely cool about the idea of meeting someone via an advertisement, a website or with the aid of some other contrived method of introduction, there'll be another who'll say the whole thing is just false. True, it won't be right for everyone – some people will never feel comfortable with the idea that they have to resort to paying out money in order to meet someone. But others will say it's the best money that they have ever spent, or the most brave and successful thing they have ever done.

You might have a laugh and a joke with your friends about it along the way, recounting stories of 'last night's dating disaster' but it's really nobody else's business but your own. Your best friend may prefer it if you were just to meet someone in a pub, and meeting someone through an advertisement is unlikely to be your first choice in how to find a partner. But life's not a rehearsal and why waste time? Countless couples will confirm how successful dating agencies and so on can be.

DATING DATA – POINTS TO REMEMBER
DATING – THE OPTIONS AND THE LINGO

→ Try to forget the stigma attached to contrived dating methods and just have some fun with it.
→ Do some homework about all the dating networks there are for single people in your area. Look at small ads in your favourite newspaper, singles' nights in your area, social clubs and other forms of arranged singles' introductions.
→ See if a single friend will come along with you to try a few different things out. It's much less scary with two!
→ Consider alternative ways of getting in touch with new people, for example speed dating, astral dating, singles' holidays and Internet dating.
→ Share your dating stories but don't let anyone else dictate how you should meet people.

8 DATING AGENCIES

The different types of dating agencies, how they work, what's involved and how much they cost.

In terms of maximising your chances of meeting your future soulmate, dating agencies are considered to be the most successful option out of all dating possibilities. Instead of whiling away the hours reading small ads, calling up pre-recorded messages or sending off on-spec letters, dating agencies go straight to the heart of the matter. They offer a way of introducing you to like-minded people and eliminate at least some of the games that people play to establish what the other person wants from a relationship.

THE ABIA

In the UK there are around 35 dating agencies belonging to the ABIA – the Association of Introduction Agencies. Member agencies follow a strict Code of Practice which is supported by the Office of Fair Trading. This means that any consumers who have problems with any ABIA member have access to various safeguards, including independent arbitration if necessary. It monitors and regulates agencies' practice and sets out a detailed code of practice for agencies to adhere to which includes:

→ **Objectives and methods of introduction (see below);**
→ **Eligibility for marriage – agencies must state if membership is restricted to people who are currently unmarried;**
→ **Criteria used for matchmaking;**
→ **Numbers of introductions, etc.;**
→ **Fees Charged;**
→ **Refunds.**

The code of practice goes to pinpoint further how the agencies must be run, how it should treat advertising and the handling of complaints, and regular random checks are made on the consumer's behalf to ensure that the agency is playing by the rules.

There are plenty of other introduction and dating agencies offering you a direct route to any number of potential dates, in whatever shape, colour or creed that you prefer. Flick through a Sunday supplement and you'll see ads for Kids No Object, Vegetarian Matchmakers, Just Woodland Friends and several other specialist agencies, so there really is something for everyone. (See the Resources section at the back of the book for further details.) Bearing in mind how expensive these very select services can be, it's a good idea to see if the agency you intend to use is a member of the ABIA. If not, see the list of Dos and Don'ts in the Dating Data section at the end of this chapter.

WHICH ROUTE TO CHOOSE?

Apart from Internet dating (see Chapter 8) there are three main types of introduction agency methods, which are:

LIST AGENCIES

This is the cheapest kind of dating agency and uses a list method. It's a kind of pen-pal service which for a one-off fee of around £30–60 will provide you with a list of members that match your criteria (in terms of age group, area and so on). The list agencies don't specifically offer any one-to-one interviews although each agency varies in its working practices. Theo Stewart runs a list agency called Singles Grapevine which at any one time has around one thousand members on its books. 'We try not to "collect" members as we hope that we've done the job and people have been matched up and move on with their lives. Therefore at Singles Grapevine we offer a basic three-month membership for £39.95 and for that we match you up with around 24 names based on your age, where you live and your profession. Then we send the details on to you by post and it's up to you to make the next move and contact them in the way that they have requested – by phone, email, post and so on. We also do a membership (price £59.95) where people are sent three lists on consecutive months so that we can select from new members who are joining all of the time.'

COMPUTER MATCHING

Dateline, the UK's biggest introduction agency, was established in 1966 and now has over 38,000 members, 40 per cent of whom are in the 30–45 year old age group. It uses the computer matching method of introduction, sorting members' compatibility by comparing their details. The applicant fills in a form, either by post or email, which includes details such as likes and dislikes, personality traits and the kind of person who they would like to meet, then the computer gets to work. Depending on how important various details are to each party, it will compare age, height, education, religion, skin colouring (for example European or southern European) whether you smoke, and so on. The computer then produces a list of details which on paper match your own details. There are no guarantees that people will be totally compatible as people's interests, needs and desires constantly change, but Dateline boasts an excellent success rate. It costs £150 for a year's membership which provides you with a one-off list of contacts, plus the opportunity for you to receive an additional list every month at a cost of £5 each. Photographs are not offered initially, but fellow members' details such as their name (could only be a first name) address, mobile number, email address or any combination of contact details can be provided.

Computer matching can obviously only be as reliable as the information which is fed into it. Therefore if you tell a few white lies on your application form or aren't specific enough about the kind of people who you would like to be introduced to, it's likely to be a waste of time for both parties.

CASE STUDY

Steven, 35 and Debbie, 34, both from South London, had reservations about joining Dateline.

Steven: *I joined Dateline at the beginning of 2001. I'm quite shy and that's always affected my chance of meeting people so I thought I'd give Dateline a go. I'd seen it advertised in newspapers and magazines and all of the success stories so I suppose it was the only one I'd ever really considered. And when they had a special offer for a free matching service I decided to send in my details. About a week* later I got six matches and I picked the person who lived nearest to me and waited for a reply. The next day I came home and did a 1471 on the phone and there was a mobile number I didn't recognise. Then the same thing happened the next night. Finally I got a call from Debbie and she sounded very lovely and we hit it off straight away. We continued to have more conversations until we both felt ready to meet up – she's really shy too so we were both really nervous about it. We met in a pub and my first thought when I saw her was, 'Wow, she's lovely!' We got on really well and we've been going out ever since. On New Year's Eve of 2001 I proposed to her and everyone thinks we're a wonderful couple together.

Debbie: *I joined Dateline in January 2001. I put in my details that I like swimming, reading, going to the cinema and socialising and when I spoke to Steven for the first time I thought he sounded lovely. We got on straight away but I was absolutely terrified the first time I met him because I thought, 'What if he doesn't like me?' but as soon as we met I instantly knew he was 'the one'. I've only told a few people how we met because I'm a bit embarrassed about it and usually tell people that we just met in a pub – they don't need to know anyway. Steven has told some of his mates and they think it's great.*

PERSONAL MATCHMAKING

The most expensive kind of introduction service, but generally considered to be the most effective, is the method of personal matchmaking, where a team of 'Cupids' compare your details with other members of the agency and match you up accordingly. The methods vary from agency to agency in how the matchmaking is achieved, but it's a much more considered approach to finding people a partner, as the agents not only know all the clients' requirements in a potential date, but can also match up personality types more effectively. And by getting feedback from their members they can further build up their knowledge of their clients for future reference.

HOW A TYPICAL DATING AGENCY WORKS

Karen Mooney set up Sarah Eden Personal Introductions in 1988 to 'remove the worry of meeting someone when you don't have much time'. 'When I first started the company I got around fifty friends and friends of friends together and we went out and recruited from there. We'd go into bars and pubs and asked people if they'd like to join for £50. Of course at that time the introduction agency wasn't a well-known concept and we were mistaken for an escort agency! After that, we used the term 'dating agency' so that people could understand what we were about and it just built up steadily from there'.

The agency now has 2,500 members and Karen has two offices in London and Windsor, plus a team of highly trained matchmakers who guide people through the various processes of becoming a member. The first point of contact is usually a phone call from a potential member who has seen an advertisement in a classified section of a magazine or maybe has heard about the agency via word of mouth. 'When someone rings up we ask them a few details such as their age, where they live and what their occupation is,' Karen explains, 'and then we send them an introduction pack outlining what the company does with details of our fees, etc.' Sarah Eden's philosophy is 'to make looking for a loving relationship an exciting adventure, possibly the greatest adventure of your life'. Members are 'intelligent, forward-thinking people who live active fulfilled lives. They know that time is precious and they trust us to make the most of it'.

After reading through the introductory blurb, new members can then make an appointment to have an interview and for security purposes they are asked to take in three forms of ID. New clients are invited to the Sarah Eden offices in Victoria where they are met by one of seven consultants who help them complete a personal profile form. 'Apart from obvious details, this has what we call "hidden" questions, such as, "What is your current refuge?" so that we can build up information as to their particular life stage.' Karen says that this is very important as the agency is aimed at people who primarily want a one-to-one monogamous relationship. 'Obviously they will meet other people along the way, but ultimately that has to be their goal.' Members then sign a confidentiality agreement so that embarrassing scenarios are avoided – such as ex-husbands and wives getting wind of their new dating arrangements!

It's at this stage that the Sarah Eden team also have to decide whether they want the person they interview actually to be on their books. It's one thing being able to afford the joining fee (which starts at £950 plus VAT for a year's membership) but not everyone is accepted, as Karen explains. 'We do have to turn people away. For example, if someone comes in and bursts into tears, you know they're not really ready to meet someone! In practical terms we have to know that we can "sell" someone – we are agents after all. So it's not fair on someone to take them on if they have unrealistic expectations. We once had a chap of 54 who only wanted to meet girls up to the age of 30. He was very wealthy and wanted to be an Executive member, but we couldn't take him on. Similarly, if people don't look after themselves, then we are going to find it hard to match them up with someone.'

Once all of the forms have been completed, the matchmakers go to work, hand-picking around 30–200 other members for the new client to look at. 'We look at various criteria, such as age, height and personal interests, and we think about how the personalities would work together.' The new client is then given a joining pack and has to supply two sets of photographs which will be shown to other members of the agency, unless they request that they want Sarah Eden's Executive membership. In this case their details aren't shown to other people, they just see other members' files and pick who they would like to contact. Once the picker has selected whom he/she would like to meet, his/her details are then sent to the pickee and if both parties are in agreement, numbers are swapped and you go on from there.

It's the matchmaker's job to cut through the files that are likely to be unsuitable matches and select potentially successful dates. 'We had to convince one man that he should see a lady who had picked him as she didn't have a particularly good photo. We just had a real feeling about the two of them and we were right as they went on to have several dates together.'

FIRST IMPRESSIONS

Obviously you should ensure that your photo shows you to your best advantage. Not that you have to go and blow your life savings on a studio shoot, just get a friend to do a whole roll of film for you, looking relaxed and happy and, hopefully, a couple of shots will fit the bill. Bear in mind professional photographers use an awful lot of film to get shots of models looking gorgeous, so be prepared to splash out on the Kodak! There's absolutely no point in looking cool, moody or posey as you'll just come across as unapproachable – which rather defeats the object. Make it a realistic impression of you though. Don't borrow someone else's 'style' for the photo session and turn up in clothes that you wouldn't normally wear and with a tan which you only got that morning. You may look fabulous, but remember that whoever you may end up meeting will expect to see the same person – more or less. Imagine if you picked a date with an Adonis and he turned up looking more like a doughnut – not a very good start really.

DATING AGENCY PACKAGES

Depending on the agency, your fee will guarantee you a certain number of 'introductions' – be they access to details of potential mates or bookings with actual dates. One of the more select London dating agencies, Only Lunch, organises a series of blind dates that they hand-pick for their clients. The lunch/early evening dinner date is booked for you and you simply turn up – and go Dutch at the end of the meal. You are not shown a photograph of the person you are going to meet, you're just told their name and occupation and have to trust the resident Cupids' judgement and go with the flow. Other agencies, such as Club Sirius and Elite, offer a home visit to get a real feel for the type of person you are before they take you on their books. Meanwhile, Drawing Down the Moon, the oldest established dating agency group, asks members to complete handwritten profiles which contain open-ended questions in order to portray a new member's cultural and lifestyle choices. Things like 'Who would you like to be in another life?' and 'Which newspapers do you take?'

EXTRA PERKS

Many companies offer you the chance of putting your membership on hold or freezing it and reactivating it up to a year later. This means that if you wanted to have a relationship with someone that you have met, you could put your multi-dating lifestyle on hold for a while. Who knows, you may never have to reactivate it again. Whichever agency you decide to go to, it's a good idea to check if an on-hold option is offered in the package otherwise you may meet someone on your first date (it could happen!) only for it all to be over eleven months later and your membership all but over too. It's also worth enquiring if there is a separate social diary drawn up by the agency – a sort of instant tailor-made social life. Many agencies (like Sarah Eden) offer a variety of members' cocktail parties and dinner dances, champagne receptions and gourmet meals, and guests are welcome at all events so you can take along a friend if you find the prospect of going alone to a party too intimidating.

THE RIGHT ATTITUDE

If you decide to use a dating agency, it's up to you to provide the most important elements to make it a success. You have to be honest with yourself, be relaxed about the whole thing and try and look upon the whole experience as a fun way to meet people, and not as a do-or-die situation. You may not instantly meet the person of your dreams, but the whole experience can help you learn more about yourself, help boost your confidence and certainly provide you with some good anecdotes! It may be expensive, but try not to take it all too seriously as you're more likely to scare off potential partners rather than endear yourself to them.

CASE STUDY

After trying and failing to meet Mr Right the conventional way, Imogen took the plunge with a whole range of dating agencies.

When I got to my early thirties I started to think that I was never going to meet anyone. I worked as a receptionist at a busy optician's but it wasn't the kind of place where you could exactly chat up the customers! A friend of mine was trying a dating agency at the time and I remember thinking, 'God, I could never do that. I'd never put myself in that kind of situation.' I once tried to chat someone up at a party and he just blanked me and after that I'd learned my lesson.

However, after much persuading, I joined a dating agency and paid £62 for a list of names of people in my area. It was incredibly nerve-wracking at first but after a while I took it all with a pinch of salt. My friends at work used to say, 'Who is it this week, Imogen?' because I'd always arrange to meet my 'dates' at the same time and the same pub, more or less the same night every week. It got to the stage where I got confused with who was who but my social life was great. I find it easy to talk to a complete stranger for a couple of hours – you can always find things to talk about of mutual interest. But a lot of the people who I dated weren't my type at all and some were absolute creeps. I remember one guy who came in with greasy hair and a centre parting wearing an anorak. As soon as he walked in he zipped his anorak up to the neck and didn't undo it for the whole of the date! At the end he said he'd love to see me again because he thought the date had really gone well!

After that I tried another agency, but I didn't get any kind of feedback and so I thought I should just put things on a back burner for a while. It's quite hard work being proactive all of the time, having to go out and project your personality and act 'like a confident person' even though I didn't feel it inside.

Some time later I saw an ad for the Sarah Eden Introduction Agency and I sent off for their brochure. When it arrived I thought it was just the Hilton Hotels of dating agencies and I thought it was much more the sort of thing that I was looking out for. My Mum said she'd help me with the joining fee and I made an appointment straight away.

The girls at the agency were lovely and after chatting to me and organising my profile, they gave me about forty sets of details to look at. I had to divide them into yes, no and maybe piles and then the girls went through my choices with me. They talked me round so that some of the 'no's became 'maybe's and then they showed my details to the people I'd picked. Funnily enough, my friend Jo was a member at that time and I liked the look of one of the guys that had been selected for her. I rang up the agency and said I'd like to meet him and although it wasn't really in the agency's rules, they put the two of us together. We had a chat on the phone and arranged to meet.

On the night Jon and I first met I had a splitting headache and I just wanted to stay in and watch Friday night TV, but I forced myself to go out in the pouring rain. I saw a guy lolling around the bar and I watched him for a while before I went up and said hello. He turned around and was so friendly that we just yakked and yakked all night. He had such a lovely friendly face and was so easy going that I thought he could end up being my best friend. At the end of the night he asked me if I wanted to meet him again and apparently (I can't remember this!) I said, 'Oh, yes! P-lease!' So we met up again and very quickly we were seeing more and more of each other. I think I started falling in love with him within the first few months. You can't wait to take someone to all of your favourite places and you find yourself planning holidays together and somehow it all happens.

We met in November 1990, spent Christmas together and in February the following year Jon proposed. We got married quickly after that and immediately started trying for a baby. After five years we decided to give IVF a try. Obviously that was a very stressful time for us and it ended up taking seven attempts for the IVF to work, but then I gave birth to twins! One of the twins unfortunately has cerebral palsy but Jon has been an absolute tower of strength and it's just made our relationship even stronger.

We'd just started to relax and enjoy our little family when I got pregnant at 42 and gave birth to a girl who's now two. So all in all Jon and I haven't really had much free time for the last few years! I wouldn't change anything for the world though.

The funny thing is that the girl who I first compared dating profiles with also married someone from a dating agency and now has two children. Not only that, my neighbour also married someone after four months who she met through a dating agency. Once you know someone who has met someone through an agency it gives you the confidence to do the same.

The best thing about dating agencies is that it narrows everything down. The people that you meet have the same interests as you, you know whether they would like to have children, what they are looking for in a relationship and so on. It's not like trying to pick someone up in a bar or a club – in those situations you may as well be looking for a needle in a haystack!

DATING DATA – POINTS TO REMEMBER
DATING AGENCIES

→ Do choose an agency which is a member of the ABIA.

→ Don't be afraid to ask how long the agency has been in business and how many members it currently has.

→ Do ensure that the people you speak to at an agency know and understand your needs and get them to explain in detail what they can do for you. Remember, you are paying them to represent you.

→ Don't be put off by agencies that ask for a lot of identification. The security measures that they employ are to protect you and your confidentiality.

→ Do visit the agency and ask to see evidence of their successful track record such as letters of recommendation, thank-you letters and wedding photographs – these are all signs that an agency knows what it is doing.

→ Don't think that you will necessarily get what you pay for. Fees vary widely from one agency to another and the most expensive is not necessarily the best.

→ Do some research on agencies in your area before you commit to anything. Don't be pushed into joining unless you feel it's the right agency for you.

→ Do check out the decor and furnishings when you visit an agency as you can tell a lot about it's success. But don't be dazzled by it, just make it part of your considered opinion process.

→ Trust your gut reaction. If you don't click with the person interviewing you, then it's unlikely that they will have got the best side of your personality either. And how are they going to be able to make a perfect match for you?

9 PLACING AN AD AND READING BETWEEN THE LINES

How you would and how you should describe yourself to your best advantage and how to choose dates that are right for you (with or without the aid of a mugshot).

When you start getting into small ads and reading people's descriptions of themselves via dating agencies and other dating avenues, you quickly get a sense of how to read between the lines and the jargon that's involved in the dating game. First there's the shorthand to figure out. It's all pretty obvious really – n/s meaning non smoker, yo – years old and so on. For the uninitiated, here are the main abbreviations:

WLTM – Would Like to Meet
GSOH –Good Sense of Humour
TLC –Tender Loving Care (whether it's being offered or needed)
OHAC – Own Home and Car
LTR – Long Term Relationship
ACA – All Calls Answered
NTW – No Time Wasters

If you are buying a property, you soon discover that 'compact and bijou' actually means 'shoebox with not enough room to swing a kitten' let alone a fully grown cat. In the same way, you can easily prune away a lot of the words in a small ad so that you can get to the heart of a small ad's profile – if indeed there is one at all. An average lonely hearts' advertisement will be around 35 words long, but of course this will vary greatly depending on the publication and the price to advertise.

AD SPEAK

When you first start to browse a lonely hearts advertising listing, the amount of choice can be quite bewildering, but you'll soon learn how to focus in on the key words of interest to you. Some ads are obviously less successful than others. This one is taken from a well-known lonely hearts' section of a London listings magazine:

WEST LONDON, professional male, 5ft 10, dark brown hair, light brown eyes, romantic, spontaneous, educated, outdoors, seeks genuine, honest, 25-40, slim, attractive female for relationship

This is a prime example of how to waste money and a great opportunity. Instead of calling himself a professional male, which can mean anything from a barrister to a dustbin man these days, this person could have used a more descriptive word about himself to show off his personality strengths, such as creative, witty, thoughtful, passionate. . . the list is endless. If you state your job it can be an instant turn-off to some people, whereas a personality type works much more in your favour. Secondly, this person should definitely have mentioned his age. Height is possibly the number one priority for women scouring the lonely hearts (more about that later) but age comes a close second. The fact that WEST LONDON is picked out in capitals right at the start of the ad is a waste too. Why not just have w/Ldn somewhere near the end? Dark brown hair, light brown eyes could have been written as dark hair and sexy eyes – someone, somewhere must think he has sexy eyes, plus it's so much more descriptive than light brown. The fact that he seeks a genuine, honest, 25–40 slim attractive female for a relationship isn't exactly a tight brief. 25–40 is a huge age group to target and how many women would really consider themselves as dishonest and not genuine? In conclusion, the majority of the ad says very little at all. However, the same person would probably get more success with this:

ROMANTIC, SPONTANEOUS, thoughtful male, 35, 5ft 10' dark hair and sexy eyes WLTM warm, slim, attractive, like-minded woman of similar age for inspiring times in the great outdoors. W/Ldn

GETTING IT RIGHT

It's very difficult to describe your personality in a nutshell without sounding cheesy or just a big fat liar. One way to crack it is to select key words that you think work well from other people's ads, then piece them together into your own character jigsaw. If you are creating an ad for yourself, it's essential to include your age and if you are advertising in a national publication, the area in which you live. Height can be defined as petite, average or tall for women as men don't tend to be as obsessed with height as women are, however the same rule doesn't apply for men. One of the case studies included in this book said he felt like an attraction at Alton Towers sometimes in terms of 'You must be this big to enjoy this ride!' When men read lonely hearts advertisements they will be more inclined to focus on colouring and build (slim, blonde, curvy, brunette and so on) but women just can't help zooming in on height.

Keep things on the light side. Even if you are a very sad, lonely, depressed person, you shouldn't be using lonely hearts to bare your soul and attract the sympathy vote. This should be a way of getting you out of yourself, moving on to happier times and allowing yourself some emotional freedom. Even if things don't end up exactly as you may have hoped in the end, you can give it your best shot, and that means starting positively.

Next, select the criteria of the person who you are hoping to attract, but be careful about your personal shopping list. Date-coach Lorraine Adams from Gorgeous Networks in London says often people have too high expectations of the kind of person they should be dating. 'People think that the world owes them a boyfriend or a girlfriend as some kind of natural right,' she says. 'But they have to be prepared that if they want the best, they also have to give the best. I tell people that if they have a wish list about how they want someone to be – how they look and behave – they have to look at themselves and ask themselves if they can match everything on that wish list. If the answer is no, then you should re-think your priorities.'

NARROWING YOUR CHOICE

If you are thinking of replying to an ad, go through a page of lonely hearts' ads with a highlighter pen and pick out the words that strike a chord with you. But be warned, 'Handsome, witty and intelligent' in real life could be 'OK-ish looking, good at knock-knock jokes and has passed a couple of GCSEs'. Just because a man says he's drop-dead gorgeous, it doesn't mean that he actually is. Get a sense for what appeals to you and what's a definite turn-off before you start diving in and replying to ads.

It's entirely up to you what you ultimately want to get out of either advertising or responding to an ad. You may be looking for someone purely with a great sense of humour, in which case don't just go for someone who describes himself as having a GSOH; see if he/she has demonstrated their humour within the ad itself. On the other hand you may want to attract someone with your GSOH or radical use of irony, but think about your wording. A flippant ad that says, 'Short, fat, ugly, skint female seeks tall, dark, handsome, rich, man,' may be totally lost on the majority of fellow lonely hearts. I should know, I ran that ad myself and didn't exactly have the best response. Self-deprecation isn't generally a good idea as some people will take it at face value. It's much better to sell yourself up and add humour into the bargain.

If you are passionate about movies or a certain sport, say so in your ad or look for someone with the same interests, which will help you narrow down your search and tailor the responses back to you. If you get bewildered by the number of ads you are reading, circle as many as you like then go back over your choices until you have a shortlist of people who you would like to meet. Around five is a safe bet to start off with.

DECISIONS, DECISIONS

Choosing a date that's right for you from lists of potentials can be a minefield. The number one rule is not to pin all your hopes on just one choice; do a bit of a pick and mix and go on from there. If you limit yourself to one person and you don't get the response you hope for then it's not going to be good for your self-esteem. Broaden your horizons. A word of warning though: remember that just because you find him/her appealing it doesn't mean that person will automatically think the same about you! A friend of mine met someone through a dating agency and thought, 'Bingo! I've met someone lovely,' and she was really quite pissed off when she discovered he didn't feel the same way. You can't assume that just because someone has contacted an agency or replied to an ad that they aren't choosy about who they meet – it's the absolute opposite in fact. They are often single for the very reason that they are incredibly choosy. And sometimes, even if you're absolutely gorgeous, you won't be good enough for someone.

SNAP HAPPY

If you are a member of a dating agency or you are trying out Internet dating, you are likely to have access to other members' photographs in order to choose potential dates. Therefore, instead of reading through hundreds of wordy descriptions, you could find yourself ploughing through books of strangers' faces. You'll probably start looking for the person who you fancy the most, but try and look further than your first impression when you are looking for a potential date. Remember, not everyone in the world is photogenic. 'Try and read the person behind the face,' says Karen Mooney from Sarah Eden Introductions. 'Try not to go 100 per cent on looks or the description in the profile, it has to be a mixture. Use your gut instinct to make choices as far as his/her personality is concerned, but be flexible about looks.'

If you are joining a dating agency or doing Internet dating, you are probably likely to have to include a photograph of yourself to run alongside your own details. If this is the case, then try and select a photograph of yourself that is a really good interpretation of how you look now. You may think that the picture someone took of you on your last night in Barbados shows off your tan really well, but be realistic – do you really look like that 99 per cent of the time? It's one thing showing yourself in a good light, but remember you'll have to live up to the image that you portray on the picture as that's what your date will be expecting to see.

REPLYING TO A VOICE ADVERTISEMENT

If you are making contact with someone who has a recorded mailbox message, don't blurt out your reply as soon as he/she has said his piece – hang up, decide what you are going to say about yourself and call back. This avoids scenarios like this: 'Oh, um, you sound really nice, don't know what to say now, oh God, this is stupid, can't believe I'm doing this. You probably aren't interested in me anyway, um, goodbye.' Keep your message light, short, focused and honest, leaving a mobile number or email address for him/her to contact you if they are interested, then hang up. This isn't the time to regale a stranger with your terrible love life track record, or pretend that you are a sex god. He/she can work that one out when and if the two of you get on further down the line.

Once you have established mutual interest with someone, it's time to take things further, but be careful. Very often the people who use lonely hearts/dating agencies have had negative experiences in the past, so it's important to take it slowly. It's important for both sides that any kind of relationship is handled safely, sympathetically and honestly.

Chapter 11 offers practical advice for dating behaviour, but before you get to that stage, you can lay the groundwork with telephone calls, emails and even the old-fashioned letter-writing method if you feel inclined. Once you've dispensed with the pleasantries, decide what kind of information you want them to know about you and what you'd like to find out about him/her. Assess how you feel about the responses they offer. Are they being cagey and secretive or maybe telling you too many intimate details that you don't really want to know at this stage? Establish a conversation either literally or via email or text-messaging, and don't feel forced to take the plunge and actually go on any kind of date until you feel totally ready. The first date can be a very nerve-wracking and emotional experience, so don't put yourself through unnecessary stress.

Texting and emailing has been a great help to the flirting/dating process. 'It's the new foreplay,' says flirting expert Peta Heskill. 'Texting is a great way to fire up the juices for steamy sex later and a healthy way of keeping the spark alive in any relationship. Unlike office email, it's a completely uncensored means of flirting between two individuals and is totally personal.' To this end, one mobile phone company has launched an entire advertising campaign on the romantic benefits of texting with the slogan, 'Get the flirting over with before you get home.' Another mobile phone company is planning a 'Flirt Alert' dating service where users can anonymously flirt with up to five people at a time, and on Valentine's Day in 2002, over eighty million romantic text messages were sent in the UK. Meanwhile over in Thailand the biggest mobile network crashed on Valentine's Day when lovers across the country went into romantic text overdrive!

THE JOY OF TEXT

Instead of having to face awkward, stilted conversations, you can now let your fingers do the talking with a few choice words – or even pictures. Swapping mobile numbers means that either party can make the move the next day with a 'I really enjoyed meeting you last night' text. Gone are the days when girls had to sit around waiting for 'him' to call – now you can just text and go.

And of course it doesn't have to end there – sending someone a picture text works well for the true romantics, meanwhile forwarding lists of jokes via email establishes your mutual sense of humour (or lack thereof). It's fun, it's relatively cheap and it takes the pressure off those crucial pre-date phone calls.

However you decide to progress your relationship with someone new, keep reminding yourself why you are doing this in the first place. If necessary, read over Chapter 3 again to work out what you want to get out of a relationship – and make sure you are not kidding yourself that you are happy with something else. Don't keep making the same mistakes again and again.

CASE STUDY

Natasha, 25, is a bilingual secretary from south London and has learned that it's not what you say in an advert, but what you neglect to say.

One of the first lessons I learned about dating agencies is that it's not so much what you tell them about yourself as what you don't tell them. I went to an agency in London and made the mistake of saying, 'I'm pretty easy going really. I'm not really worried about what people do for a living,' only to be paired up with a World War II enthusiast who had very right-wing political opinions and collected model tanks as a hobby. He fitted all the criteria that I had feebly requested – he was tall, fairly good looking, into fitness and was very intelligent – but the date was a disaster. He had obviously said he was 'pretty easy going' too, and he was obviously as unhappy with the date as I was. You go along in life thinking that your social peers are quite similar to you and I suppose on the whole they are because when you're at university or in a certain job or social circle you tend to mix with the same crowd. You take it for granted that someone of the same age who may have similar 'single' circumstances to you may not be so totally different.

I've learned that I am actually very picky about social morality and that politics is much more important to me than I thought it was. After the date I called the agency to give them some feedback as they had requested and they changed the details on my file accordingly. My second date was much more my kind of thing, but again I discovered that I had to add further criteria to my list. I'd forgotten to say I hate cigar smoke. . .

As you get older (and wiser) you don't get more desperate for a date, but much more choosy and you soon find that the people that you meet up with on dates – especially people who sign up with dating agencies – are much more choosy too. I made another mistake of arrogantly thinking that a person I met up with was good enough to meet up with for a second date (and maybe more) but he'd already made up his mind that I didn't actually cut the mustard for him. You automatically assume (or at least, I did) that people who are on dating agency books are a bit desperate and dateless, but it's just not true. They're just a hell of a lot more picky. After all, why would a tall dark and handsome, witty, successful and intelligent man be using the services of a dating agency? They are out there, but now I know that I can't assume I'll be 'the one' they're looking for.

DATING DATA – POINTS TO REMEMBER
PLACING AN AD AND READING BETWEEN THE LINES

→ If you are creating an ad, select words from other people's ads which strike a chord with you.

→ Describe yourself to your best advantage, and don't forget your age and locality.

→ Don't bother stating the obvious and try to be creative – but not cheesy.

→ When you are replying to ads, don't just reply to one – keep your options open and reply to half a dozen or so.

→ If you are finding it hard to narrow down a selection, look for key words that make you tick such as 'sporty', 'thoughtful' and so on.

→ Look beyond a photograph and use your gut instinct to decide on a date.

→ Plan voice mailbox messages before you leave them.

- → Take everything one step at a time. Don't arrange to meet someone unless you feel good about it.
- → Try a little email and text flirting instead of tackling potentially nerve-wracking phone calls.
- → Keep reminding yourself what you want to get out of a date/relationship.

10 GETTING A DATE 'THE HARD WAY'

How to use flirting, body language, confidence tricks and practical advice when you don't have the back-up of a dating service.

Setting aside for a moment dating agencies, lonely hearts and all of those dating services that cut to the chase of why you want to meet someone, how do you go about getting a date when you meet someone at a party, in the pub or a club? It's like sales people having to 'cold call' customers. How do you seal the deal? How do you turn that chance glance across the dance floor into the first date? By now you should be armed with plenty of body language and confidence tricks to be giving off the right signals, but what are the other ways that you can make the best first impressions?

WATCH WHAT YOU WEAR

Your clothes are a part of your personality, so be careful about the signals that they are giving off. OK, so you may be in a very hot night club and need to keep cool, but if you are just wearing a string bikini (I'm mostly talking to the girls here) it stands to reason that you'll be seen as someone who's very confident and self-assured. And that may actually be quite intimidating to a guy. If you are wearing a very busty top, come-and-get-me shoes and dramatic make-up, then you will come over as a bit of a vixen whether you like it or not. Similarly, if you wear frumpy librarian's shoes, a 'sensible' length skirt and a long-sleeved high-necked blouse, then you are using your clothes as a barrier. Even if you don't mean to, you are giving off signals that you are untouchable – even though you may be a complete nymphomaniac under all of those layers.

We all have our favourite clothes and things that we think suit us down to the ground, but sometimes you have to step away from yourself and really analyse what your clothes say about you. If you need any more convincing, the next time you are on a bus, in a supermarket or any other public place, have a look at a person's shoes and see how much you can evaluate from them.

Ask yourself:
How worn are they?
How clean are they?
Are they in need of a bit of TLC?
Do they make a statement about the person?

Now try and build up a picture of the rest of that person's life simply based on their shoes. What do you think their home is like? What do you think their attitude is to life generally? If you can read all of that information simply by looking at a pair of shoes, then imagine how many more signals your total style package is giving off.

That's why it's so important – for both men and women – to wear clothes that reflect your personality. You may think that the Homer Simpson tie is a good idea or your Donald Duck cuff links are quite cute, but if you truly believe you're a sex god then your accessories aren't doing you any favours, are they?

WHO ARE YOU TRYING TO ATTRACT?

Think about the kind of person you would like to date. Remember that shopping list of requirements that you might have about the person that you want to meet? If you want to meet some someone über-stylish, then you have to pull out all the stops as far as your own dress sense is concerned. You have to try and match up to the person who you want to attract. Similarly, if you would like to meet a high-flying city type, then you have to think of who they in turn would like to be seen with. Date coach Lorraine Adams from Gorgeous Networks identifies this type as 'cash rich, time poor'. 'This type of man is much more assertive about what he wants and will definitely go for looks and appearances rather than strong minds and good personalities because he will probably feel as though he has that ground covered. In this cash rich, time poor existence, he's more interested in a woman's looks – especially if he is doing well for himself and he can afford to surround himself with beautiful things. Even the ones who aren't very good looking will go more on face value.'

But no matter how flash you are with the cash, the majority of people would prefer to be liked on the merit of their personality rather than their bank balance and as much as you may want to, you can't buy genuine affection. Keep reminding yourself what you want to find in a date then take a long hard look at yourself in the mirror and, if you dare, ask a friend's opinion about whether they think you make the grade.

BE A CREATURE OF HABIT

Even if you don't join any clubs, sign up for any courses or hang around the supermarket on singles' night, you can still increase your chances of meeting people by making yourself a creature of habit. When we were at school we regularly saw people we fancied at the same place and time, whether it was at the bus stop, at the local park or in a café that you'd go to with friends. Remember how you used to make a habit of going there just in case 'he/she' would be there? Making yourself a 'regular' at a certain bar or café also increases your chances of meeting more people and maybe sparking up a romance. If you go to the same place on the same night of the week every week, there's a chance that you'll get to recognise other regulars after a while so you have the opportunity at least to build up an eye-contact relationship. If you hate going to bars, try doing the supermarket shopping at the same time, getting into a regular routine at the gym or walking in the park at the same time every Saturday morning.

MAKE YOURSELF APPROACHABLE

People meet in all sorts of different circumstances, not just pubs, clubs and parties. Whether it's at the bus stop, an evening class or standing next to the photocopier at the office, the actual location where you meet someone shouldn't really matter, although some places are obviously going to be more conducive to romance than others. The important thing is that if another person feels that they want to take the plunge and introduce themselves to you, they won't feel intimidated by what's going on around you.

When you go out with your friends, be sure to separate yourself from them occasionally. The thought of being turned down in front of a crowd of people will certainly scare off potential admirers, so nobody is going to approach you if you are surrounded by your cronies. Date coach Lorraine Adams says that the ideal number of friends to go out with if your sole intention is to pick people up or be picked up is two others. 'That way, if someone wants to approach you, the other two can talk to each other and they won't have to face an intimidating barrage of people.'

The simple way to make yourself approachable is to make sure you look friendly. Sitting looking cool may look sexy but it certainly isn't very inviting and you will be giving off 'untouchable' signals. Ask friends to give you feedback on how approachable you seem to be. Keep checking your body language and avoid signals that say 'Go away loser – I'm not interested!' And keep practising those flirting techniques. Remember what practice makes.

WATCH YOUR MANNERISMS

A huge gaggle of girls laughing loudly and throwing themselves around may be great fun to be part of, but it looks like a nightmare from virtually every other angle. A survey on attraction carried out by Gorgeous Networks concluded that women who are over-animated are a major turn-off. If you laugh loudly at your own jokes, squeal with delight about something or just shout with enthusiasm, your high spirits can quickly be misinterpreted as aggressive confidence which is going to be a turn-off to that intimidated alpha male.

Similarly guys, watch how you come across. You may think it looks macho to guffaw at rugby jokes, slap each other on the back, burp and fart, but there are very few ladies who will find it a turn-on. If they do, do you really want to be with a farting admirer? If you're out on the pull with the lads but actually would like to meet someone for more than a one-night stand, then check your actions, your body language and your mates. You can read an awful lot about a person by the company that they keep, so consider the signals that your friends are giving off about you. I'm not suggesting that you ditch all of your old buddies, just bear in mind it's not just you that the ladies are looking at.

MAKING A MOVE

According to flirt coach Peta Heskill, 95 per cent of the men she has surveyed would love women to make the first move and approach them, instead of women always assuming (and hoping) that men will make the first move. 'Making the first move doesn't have to become a habit,' she says 'and it doesn't have to be a *Sex and the City* type of approach. It's just an alternative way of doing things. If you see someone across the room that "does something for you", connect with that person and follow your instincts. Many of us don't listen to our deeper instincts and miss out on wonderful opportunities.'

It's not the best opener in the world to walk up to someone and say, 'Do you come here often?' but everyone can instantly boost their appeal and potential for success with a simple smile and a hello. Depending on where you are at the time you can always find something to talk about (see Chapter 4) but as confident as you might be about talking to someone, what you ultimately should be working towards is a productive conversation. So ask open-ended questions that require more than yes/no answers, be friendly, non-threatening and try a little sparkly flirting. You could always say, 'Do you mind me asking what kind of aftershave you wear? It's amazing,' which not only compliments the person, but shows your sensual side. If you are a smoker, you could ask to borrow a lighter and strike up a conversation from there. Or if you are in a club you could ask someone about the DJ, if they know what time the club shuts and if there is anywhere near to get good coffee and so on. Smile, be friendly and happy and you'll help to put other people at ease.

GETTING THE TIMING RIGHT

According to dating experts you should give yourself twenty minutes to get to know someone initially. The first five minutes you will be both taking in each other's physical appearances and that's why speed dating works on a very physical, 'do I fancy him/her?' level. In that five minutes you are taking in their body language, clothes, looks, sound of voice, flirting technique and so on. The next five minutes you automatically divert to what is going on around you and set yourself in the surroundings – talk about the bar you are in and who you are with. Then the next ten minutes you start to find out about each other more specifically – what line of work you are both in, whether you live locally, what you are into and so on. If you are speed dating of course, you may not have twenty minutes to evaluate the other person, but then you may only be interested in looks anyway.

If you are either chatting someone up or being chatted up, twenty minutes is the 'golden time' for you to spend with someone. Even if you are having the time of your life, it's better to break away from there as that gives the potential for either of you to start to 'seal the deal'. You could say, 'I've really enjoyed talking to you, if you are around I'd love to meet up for a coffee with you,' and if that seems to go down well you can say, 'What's your number?' Bingo!

However, if you have been bored rigid by the other person you initially approached, or if he/she has just waltzed up and started talking to you, don't feel bad about being the first to break away. Once you feel sure in yourself that you have had the chance to get to know each other and decide if you'd like it to go any further, then seal the deal – either make/encourage the next move or move on.

DATING DATA – POINTS TO REMEMBER
GETTING A DATE 'THE HARD WAY'

→ Choose clothes wisely and analyse what they say about your personality.
→ Think about who you want to attract and make sure that you match up to your own shopping list of requirements.
→ Make yourself a 'regular' at certain places.
→ Try and be approachable and watch your mannerisms and body language.
→ (For women) Consider making the first move.
→ Say hello and smile.
→ Try a little flirting.
→ After twenty minutes, walk away or 'seal the deal'.

11 TAKING THE PLUNGE – THE FIRST DATE

*Practical advice on date behaviour from safety tips to
conversational no-nos.*

So, you've decided to take the plunge and go on a date with someone
without having physically met them before. It may be someone who
you have met through a dating agency, in which case you may
already know what the person looks like and you may have built up a
rapport with them over the telephone. But whether you are going on
a blind date with a friend of a friend, meeting up with someone who
you have met online or possibly just having a date with someone
from work, learning the rules of safe dating is crucial. They may
apply to women more than men, but there's no reason why men
shouldn't take the information on board. It may also help you realise
why women seem very cagey when you first meet them. We're like
that because in this day and age we have to be.

Just because you like the sound of someone on the phone, fancy
the mugshot you've seen of them online or enjoyed being chatted
up by them in a crowded club, it doesn't mean that you are totally
safe with someone. Unfortunately there are a lot of untrustworthy
people out there and some very strange things can happen on
dates, so it's worth taking on board some practical advice. Dating
websites, dating books and just about anyone who claims to know
something about dating will immediately tell you the golden rules.

BEFORE THE DATE

Don't give away too much information. Keep your personal details
to yourself in terms of where you live, your home number and
precise work details. Your first impression of someone may be that
they are absolutely fine, but if the date doesn't work out and you've
given away too many details about yourself, things could become a
bit tricky if he/she won't take no for an answer. People can be very
persistent. Remember *Fatal Attraction*? OK, so it's unlikely that
someone will actually go to those extremes, but the character that

Glenn Close played looked like an uncomplicated person, but she didn't like to take no for an answer and look what happened there!

Keep details vague. Obviously you can't be so secretive that the person thinks you've got something to hide, but be sensible. In fact, you don't have to tell people any more than your first name if you don't want to. Let's face it, giving someone your name, address, home and mobile phone number and work details looks a bit desperate so keep an air of mystery about yourself.

Before the date, try role-playing to calm your nerves. 'Literally rehearse how you are going to greet him/her and the way you are going to behave,' says dating agent Mary Balfour from Drawing Down the Moon. 'This could be just in your mind, in front of the mirror, or with a friend. You may feel a bit foolish doing it at the time, but you'll be amazed at the difference it can make to the date and how much more relaxed you are likely to feel. Also always remember to have a conversation *with* somebody and not at somebody.'

TELL YOUR FRIENDS

Give one of your friends the details of where you are going on your date, plus the person's name, phone number and any other details that you think are relevant. It's a good idea to tell your friend that you will call them after an hour or so to let them know that things are OK. If you want to be more subtle about it, you could tell your date that you have to make a quick call and use some honest-sounding excuse like key arrangements with a neighbour. Then call your friend to let them know that you're OK. Or if you have a mobile, maybe you could ask them to give you a quick call. It might sound extreme but with so many horror stories in the press about people being assaulted by people that they know, not to mention strangers, you need to take extra care.

PLAN SHORT DATES

If you're planning your first date, arrange to meet someone you've never met before for a cup of coffee, or a quick bite for lunch rather than a full-on dinner in the evening. Not only is this much safer, because it's more likely to be in daylight, but if it's a lousy date it stops you both wasting your time. You are also less likely to drink too much at lunchtime or be carried away by the romantic surroundings of a candlelit supper, which may seem very different in the cold light of day. If you really like someone, you can plan a different kind of date for the second time you meet up and go on from there.

KEEP IT PUBLIC

Make sure you plan your date where there are a lot of people around. Go to busy places, preferably where you are known and make sure you chat to the waiter/waitress while you are there. If the worst comes to the worst and your date becomes a nightmare, you will have established some kind of support mechanism to deal with it. Psychologically you'll feel more in control and in very extreme cases you'll have a witness in case things get really out of hand. This may all sound like scare-mongering but certainly as far as women are concerned, it's just good common sense. We can all get swept away by romantic gestures and want to throw caution to the wind, but sometimes you just have to take a step back and review the situation. Nobody wants to be another statistic or have their name mentioned in the same sentence as a date-rape story.

TRUST YOURSELF

Listen to your heart and trust your gut reaction as to whether something/someone is a good idea. Most of us know immediately whether a date is a complete mistake within the first ten minutes of meeting someone, so why drag it out longer than necessary? If you hear alarm bells from the start, don't ignore them. Remember, you are in control of who you choose to spend time with and it's perfectly reasonable for you to politely decline an invitation or tell someone (kindly) that they're not the kind of person who you are looking for. Simply finish your coffee, or your lunch, smile and say, 'Well, it was really nice to meet you. I've actually got to meet someone in half an hour, so shall we settle up the bill?' Hopefully they will have already got the message through your body language and conversation that you are not interested in seeing them again.

But if they pursue the subject you can say, 'I'm sorry, but I don't think this is completely what I'm looking for at the moment, but it was good to meet you.' You're being honest, it was good to meet them – if only to realise that they are not your kind of date material and to tighten up your criteria for your next date. Just put it down to experience and move on.

HOME ALONE

If you have a great date, as tempting as it may be, don't accept any lifts, go back to a stranger's house or invite them back to your home when you have only just started to get to know them. This has nothing to do with The Rules, playing hard to get or taking the moral high ground, it's purely for safety's sake. You may have got on like a house on fire and been treated with the utmost respect on the date, but sadly there's no guarantee that this will continue further into the night. There's a slim chance that things could become unpleasant, so why risk it at all? If things have gone really well on the first date, just enjoy it and look forward to the next. Why rush things? There are people who enjoy one-night stands and have their own views on safety, but whatever your views are on casual sex, use common sense and be safe.

TALKING POINTS

Hmmm, what should you talk about on a first date? Flirting, dating and relationships experts have various views on the subject because it tends to depend on the manner in which you met your date and what you eventually want to get out of it. Whether you are going on a casual date or whether you are trying to meet a long-term partner, you'll want to get things off to the best possible start.

SCENARIO ONE: AGENCY DATING

If some serious Cupid work has been going on before the first date and the two of you have been matched up by a dating agency, the Internet, or by whittling down lonely hearts, then the chances are that you will already know quite a few details about each other. For example, you are more likely to know if the person has been married before, if he/she has any children, what their job is, what their likes and dislikes are and so on. You may have exchanged emails, talked on the phone or even got into some text flirting prior to the date, so you will have laid some of the foundations before you even meet. The chances are that you'll have an idea of what both of you would like the outcome of the date to be – whether you are meeting someone just for a one-off night out or looking for something seriously long term.

Mary Balfour, head of the Drawing Down the Moon group of dating agencies, holds singles' seminars on the right and wrong ways to go about dating. With her experience as unofficial Head Cupid at Drawing Down the Moon, she advises on what to say – and more importantly, what not to say – on a first date. Although it may seem tempting to blast in and start asking questions about ex-lovers, Mary says it's the number one no-no. 'The general rule is don't ask and don't talk about your own relationships,' says Mary. But that doesn't mean to say that you shouldn't find out about their relationship history. 'If you haven't already established whether someone has ever been married or has any children, then you should get the facts about their relationship history, but you don't need to dwell on the intricacies of it. Establish what the person you are with wants to get out of the date itself and that way you can avoid wasting each other's time. If you meet someone and they want something totally different to you, for goodness sake don't just go along with it, hoping that you may be able to change them into what you want by some kind of romantic osmosis. It just won't happen.' That doesn't mean to say that you start the conversation, 'Fancy getting married?' but you can talk about where you are 'at' at this point in your life and how you would eventually like to see your life in the future.

Although you can look at dating as a fact-finding mission, make sure it doesn't turn into the Spanish Inquisition! You don't want to go along with a list of questions because it sounds as if you're interrogating someone and it can really wind them up! 'I don't give people recipes of subjects to talk about, it's more about finding out what the other person is interested in and talking to them about their interests,' Mary says. 'It's important to ask them what they feel and think about things and keep it on a more emotional level, rather than asking them factual questions such as what they do exactly for a living.'

'It may seem strange,' says Mary, 'but politics is actually a very good subject to talk about on a first date. It helps you establish so much about a person and their views on life.' If someone has totally different political leanings to you and different values on society, then its likely to disrupt your relationship further down the line. We can all pretend to be liberal minded about each other's views, but if you are diametrically opposed to your partner's way of thinking, it can only cause conflict eventually. In terms of religious beliefs, however, Mary says 'datees' should be more cautious. 'It's really a subject to be avoided on the first date – depending on how important it is for you as far as relationships are concerned. However, if it is really important for you to meet someone of the same faith, then you are likely to have established that criteria from the outset.'

People are understandably nervous on a first date and if there's a gap in the conversation, women especially seem to feel the need to fill it. It's a much better idea to hold back on what you tell someone on a first date. 'Show vulnerability, yes, but don't tell someone everything about you,' Mary says. 'Take it *slowly*; by rushing it you'll only scare someone off immediately.'

As part of her Singles' Seminars, Mary covers ways that you can reduce nervousness with good breathing techniques. And along with body language and role playing you can make yourself much more prepared for a first date. 'All in all,' says Mary, 'you have to strike a balance between finding out information about someone and letting them know about you, and a lot of the success of the date is down to how good you feel about yourself. If you go into a date feeling confident (but not cocky) then you'll do yourself justice.'

SCENARIO TWO: MORE 'CASUAL' DATING

If you are on a blind date, trying speed dating or on a much more 'casual' date (where paying a middleman to do the matching doesn't come into the equation), you can afford a more casual approach to conversation and the date itself. Date coach Lorraine

Adams confirms that the most common mistake that anyone makes on a first date is talking too much. 'I find that if people aren't used to dating – perhaps if they have just come out of a long relationship or if they don't date that often – they plough straight into the conversation and don't leave anything out. But the most intriguing thing about meeting someone is keeping a bit of mystery. The idea is to be a bit evasive and leave them not knowing too much about you. More importantly, leave them wanting to know more about you because what they have heard so far is so intriguing. If you are constantly answering all their questions and giving them a bit more as well, it spoils the excitement.'

'In order to stop telling someone too much, you can put the brakes on,' says Lorraine. 'When they say to you, "Tell me about yourself," say, "Oh, no, I'd like to know about you." Or if you find yourself going into a long-winded conversation, just say, "Hey, I'm going to quit while I'm ahead here, let's talk about you," thereby deflecting the conversation back to them.'

If you are on a date and find yourself stuck for words but don't want to get into anything 'heavy' such as what your long-term emotional plans are for life, you could make a reference to something that is happening around you. 'If you are in a bar, talk about other people around you and pick up on their mannerisms,' Lorraine advises. 'Then you are deflecting the emphasis off the two of you as a couple and can have a laugh and giggle rather than talking intently about yourselves.

'It's always better to talk about the status quo than to talk about your past relationships,' says Lorraine. 'Talk about what you like and don't like by all means, but don't go too far into letting them know too much about you. As a guide I tell my clients that you should give them 20 per cent on the first date. They really don't need to know how many boyfriends or girlfriends you've had, don't go too deep.'

According to Lorraine, the most common mistake that men repeatedly make on a first date is that they are too boastful. 'Women don't want to know that he's got a Porsche outside. What we want is to see him nonchalantly getting into his Porsche at the end of the date. That's much more impressive. Similarly, we don't want to know how much money he has, the countries he has travelled to and where he buys his clothes, but that's what men think that women want to hear.' Of course, there will be plenty of single women out there that will be very turned on with the idea of the Porsche, the five-star holidays, the Gucci suits and the expense account, but after a while surely even the biggest gold-diggers must get sick of it?

'We did a survey on our members and found out that although people find confidence attractive, people forgive a bit of nervousness and it's quite endearing.' Lorraine also says that loud behaviour, loud laughing and over-animated gestures are an instant turn-off. 'The golden rule is don't get drunk just to combat your nerves. It just can't be forgiven and there's nothing worse than a drunk girl or guy on the first date. Just be yourself and if the chemistry isn't there then there's no point in pretending to be someone you're not just to please someone else. It'll all go sour in the end.'

THE PRACTICAL STUFF

It may sound obvious but if you are going on a date you should really try and make some kind of effort to look good. Put it this way, if you were going to sell your car, you'd make sure it was gleaming and looked its best, so treat yourself with the same respect. 'My advice is to go all out,' says Lorraine. 'If you have a high wish list of expectations from the date, then go all out to make yourself look the best you can. If you are a woman who's not very tall, there are things that you can do to make yourself appear taller, or you can pick up on other aspects of yourself that you are proud of. If you are little overweight and could never be slim in a million years, wear clothes that suit your figure.' It should also go without saying that you should make sure that you are clued up about personal hygiene and that you try to be as well groomed as possible. 'That means clean nails and no dirty shoes!' says Mary Balfour. It's no guarantee that your date will be any more successful than it was ever going to be, but if nothing else, it will give you the confidence that you look your best and that you are not letting yourself down.

It may be tempting to make your date feel as special as possible in terms of where you go and what you do, but don't do anything which will make you feel intimidated or obliged to wear clothes that you don't really feel comfortable in. If you can't walk in a pair of shoes or if your trousers are so tight that they outline your last meal, then do yourself a favour and go for a different option. Even if you are going to a swanky Dinner Dates ball, you can still feel completely comfortable about what you are wearing. Remember, there's no point in trying to be someone who you are not – no matter how glamorous you think you look at the time.

As you get more experienced (or make more mistakes) you will learn how you can make dating better. From how to handle difficult conversations, to what to do if your date has terrible table manners or starts groping you under the table, the main tip that you can arm yourself with is to stay in control. Whether this means watching your drinking or simply not telling someone your life story, keep on top of the dating situation and always stay one step ahead. Not only will it maximise the success of the date, it will ensure that neither of you waste your time and most importantly of all that you stay safe.

For all the importance that we all put on a first date, Mary Balfour from Drawing Down the Moon says all single people should keep an open mind about their first date experiences. 'Don't judge someone on the first date,' she says. 'Try and judge a relationship by the friendship that you have with someone. Anyone can feel lust and attraction, but you have to recognise it as such and realise that a more substantial relationship needs more substance to it. If you feel you could conceivably have a long-term friendship with someone then you could have a long-term relationship with them as long as the chemistry is there. If the possibility of friendship isn't there from the start, you should just kill it dead.'

If you are in the London area and feel that you would like some one-to-one date coaching of your own, Lorraine Adams's company, Gorgeous Networks, charges £45 for an initial hour's date coaching consultation to check your dating techniques. Then if you want to take the plunge and have your approach to dating examined in more detail, Lorraine sets you up with two dummy dates. After the first one she talks to both parties and builds up a dossier of your dating techniques and then discusses it with you. The next step is to put all of your new-found knowledge into practice in a second date and then the interview process is repeated. 'I'll tell you what your best friends won't!' says Lorraine, so if you're feeling brave and want to get your dating technique totally perfected, then the one-to-one approach could be for you. For more information, see the Resources section at the back of the book.

CASE STUDY

35-year old Ellen from Leamington Spa was determined she'd have a date for Valentine's Day.

I put an ad in a lonely hearts column of a magazine once and was intrigued to hear from someone who called himself a 'Piscean sex therapist'. His photo looked OK so I gave him a call and we seemed to click immediately. I don't know which one of us was flirting more over the phone, but I don't remember asking him any particularly relevant questions. I just got swept up in the whole ego-boost of the situation. Very quickly we decided to make a date – on Valentine's Day night would you believe, and before he called off he asked me to tell him my star sign.

Valentine's Day arrived and very nervously I met up with my blind date. He was nice looking (but then I'd seen his photo so I knew he would be) and he was very well groomed which I appreciated. As soon as we sat down – after he had been very edgy with the waitress for not letting us have the exact table he wanted – he proceeded to tell me he'd done a compatibility chart for the two of us. He then went on to say he'd analysed it with his mum – whom he still lived with (he was 44). It was at this point I started to hear alarm bells in my head and regretted not finding out a bit more about him on the phone before we committed to a date. Then, stealing myself, I asked him what exactly he did for a living to which he replied that he helped others explore different sexual possibilities. Now I'm not a prude by any means, but when he started to compound the joys of a very bizarre practice (that to my mind belonged in the toilet, not the bedroom) I just resigned myself to another lost Valentine's night. At the end of the evening he got up and snorted, 'I think that went rather well, don't you?' and told me he'd call me the next day. I had stupidly given him my work number, so the next day he called five times and I was very worried he'd get the office address from the receptionist and just turn up with a bunch of flowers (or a toilet roll, or something). Luckily the receptionist always asks who's calling so I could avoid talking to him.

That evening I decided I had to nip this one in the bud. I called him and said I'd enjoyed meeting him but, to be honest, it wasn't the relationship for me, at which he sounded quite crestfallen. I finished the phone call by saying, 'It was great meeting you, good luck in the future,' but I couldn't hang up quickly enough. I then ran around my flat going, 'Arghhhh!'

I realise with hindsight that my initial flirty conversation could have lead him on and the fact that I didn't try and find out anything major about him – like what he did for a living – was even more daft. You learn from your mistakes and now I know from the outset that you have to find out as much as you can about a person before you meet them and make sure your first date is (sometimes mercifully) short. I'll think twice about giving out my work number again too.

DATING DATA – POINTS TO REMEMBER
TAKING THE PLUNGE – THE FIRST DATE

→ Before the date, try and get to know him/her on the phone or by email before you agree to meet up. Practise how you will greet him/her and your opening conversation.

→ Meet somewhere public and plan a quick first date such as a coffee, or a quick lunch.

→ Do yourself a favour and make sure you look your best.

→ Tell a friend where you are going and consider calling them mid-date for a progress report.

→ Listen to your heart and trust your gut reactions about someone.

→ Don't talk too much or give away too much about yourself.

→ Ask your date what he/she 'thinks' and 'feels' about things rather than interrogating them about their life history.

→ Ensure that you both have the same relationship goals.

→ Don't brag or be too self-deprecating.

→ Consider how far you want the first date to go and be on top of the situation.

→ Keep an open mind about all of your dating experiences and try and learn from them.

12 BEYOND THE DATE

Taking things further, understanding the importance of your own pace as well as other people's. How to use dating experiences positively to learn more about yourself generally.

What happens after your first date with someone very much depends on how successful (or otherwise) the date was and how you handled it at the time. If it was a complete disaster and you really never should have even stepped out of your front door, then it's relatively simple to know how to deal with it. The chances are that your date also felt your first encounter didn't go so well, or you ended the evening with, 'Well, it was nice to meet you and I had a great time but I don't think we're ideally suited to each other.' You can brush the experience under the carpet and get on with life – maybe with a few giggles with your mates about your disastrous date along the way.

One thing's for sure, terrible dates have great comedy value. One of my friends told me a great blind-date story where she met a guy called Simon whose opening gambit was to tell her that he'd actually changed his name by deed poll to 'Tiger' because it brought out the animal side in him. Now this guy was barely five foot nine – not that that should be important, let's not be shallow here – but he had a body like the guy from the Mr Muscle ad and a voice like David Beckham's. The date itself was actually quite nice – good food in a nice restaurant and so on – but it soon became clear that this guy was actually slightly unhinged as he poured out his life story over the course of the next seven hours. My friend was utterly drained by the end of it but, if nothing else, she has got a great stand-up routine out of it – obviously with a couple of exaggerations along the way for extra laughs.

The point is that as long as you are sensible about the dos and don'ts of dating and the security side of meeting total strangers, then dating should actually be about having fun. Not to the extent where you're just going out with a series of extras from *One Flew Over the Cuckoo's Nest*, but where you are going out and meeting new friends and learning a lot about yourself along the way. By allowing yourself to be open to new romantic possibilities you are also allowing yourself to be open to new ideas and ways of thinking. When you get to the age of eighteen you may technically be classed as an adult but we all keep growing up the older and wiser we get.

As for what happens next with a date, if the two of you got on really well but there was no chemistry there, then you should still consider swapping addresses and think whether some of your other single mates might like an introduction. The important thing is to use each date positively and move on. Turn bad experiences into great anecdotes, lukewarm experiences into possible potentials for other mates or great first dates into the start of something even greater.

WORST-DATE SCENARIOS

Unfortunately it's not always so cut and dried. There are always dates where one person is much keener than the other and sometimes no amount of hint dropping that you're not remotely interested has any effect. If towards the end of the date you tried out the 'ditch the date' line and it fell on deaf ears, then you are likely to have more of a problem – especially if you broke the first-date rule and told him/her where you live and/or work. You may find yourself bombarded with phone calls, text messages or, heaven forbid, unexpected visits, so that's why *it's absolutely crucial* never to tell someone your home address until you feel totally happy about the situation. Obviously, if you have met someone through a reputable dating agency, they are likely to have been positively vetted by agency staff and so you can at least report any misgivings you may have about them, but it's best to avoid the situation entirely if you can.

Nearly all of us know of someone who is totally sane, confident and sussed on the surface, but who turns into an amateur stalker/ nuisance caller/soppy texter when they've drunk too much – and sometimes even when they are completely sober. That's why it's so important to tell it how it is if you feel that something isn't a good idea. Don't string someone along if you don't like him or her and say 'I'll call you, let's do it again,' when you have absolutely no intention of doing so. Just be straight about it. It may seem the harder option at the time but you'll be glad you did in the long run. Be kind and tactful, but don't build up someone's hopes if you have absolutely no intention of ever seeing them again. That's just plain rude – and cruel.

If you are at the receiving end of the 'ditch the date' line, however well you thought the date went, if that opinion wasn't mutual then there's really no point getting stressed about it or thinking that you can change someone's mind about you. When someone says, 'I really like you, but I'd like to stay just friends,' it means just that. Accept it for the fact that someone who you really like wants to cultivate a friendship with you, but understand that it doesn't mean, 'Let's be friends and then maybe one day I might fancy you and change my mind.' If there isn't the initial spark between two people, it's highly unlikely that things will ever change. True, there are the *When Harry Met Sally* scenarios when two people who have known each other for ages finally get together but, as if you need reminding, *When Harry Met Sally* was a movie and in real life things tend to be a bit different. The number of single men and women who go around mooning after their friends and wishing that it could be something more just isn't funny. (I should know, I've done it enough.)

USING A MIDDLE MAN (OR WOMAN)

The great thing about dating via a dating agency is it's so cut and dried. If you don't get the message about whether he/she liked you on the date or vice versa, one phone call to the agency 'Cupid' will set the record straight. You can simply ring them up, give them your feedback and ask to hear theirs. If it's negative either way you'll get to know, and you can move on from there. Simple. 'We matchmakers are very very good at our jobs and it's our business to know about our members,' says Mary Balfour from Drawing Down the Moon. 'It's part of our job to get feedback from members on how a date went and tell each other about our clients. That way we can multiply members' opportunities to meet the right people.' Dating services may be seen as less romantic than chance encounters but they can cut out a lot of the time-wasting wishing, waiting and hoping stages.

HANGING ON THE TELEPHONE

At some time or another, every single female on the planet and quite a few of the male species (if they admit it) must have sat down by their telephone or stared at their mobile phone willing it to ring. When someone says, 'I'll call you,' and then doesn't, it's one of the most frustrating things in the world – especially when you are really keen on them. Traditional etiquette tells us that it should be the man who makes the call, but as a huge percentage of the male population tends to be phone-phobic, women sometimes have to turn a blind eye to etiquette. The simplest way for a female to avoid hanging on the telephone is to put herself in the driving seat and just tell her date that she'll call him. It's not only empowering but it's safer than giving out your telephone number to a stranger. If he says he'll call you, say, 'Actually I'm having trouble with my phone at the moment and may have to change the number, so give me yours and I'll ring you.'

If you find yourself in the situation that you have left things up in the air, and you're waiting for him/her to call you and he/she doesn't, then put it down to experience and move on. Whether or not you agree with all of the tried and tested dating techniques in *The Rules* by Ellen Fein and Sherrie Schneider, the two experts have a piece of advice that everyone would do well to take on board. 'If he does not call, he's not interested. Period.' And it works the other way around. If you're a man waiting for a woman to call you and she doesn't, she's not interested. As much as you might like to convince yourself that the other person lost your number or has been incapacitated in some way and has lost the ability to use the phone in a freak accident, you're just deluding yourself. Sorry, but they just don't want to know. And for goodness sake, do yourself a favour and don't call them. If they have truly lost your number but they're still keen to get in contact with you, they'll find a way.

DEALING WITH REJECTION

Being rejected after the first date or further on into the relationship can only be a negative and it's hard to turn around and stoically say, 'Oh well, it's all down to fate at the end of the day.' But look at it logically and you only really have two options. You can make yourself feel even more miserable about it or you can just deal with it and move on. Have a good cry and/or a rant with your best friend about what's happened by all means, but try to look at the situation laterally.

If this relationship ended the same way as any of your other relationships, then analyse where you think it may have gone wrong and make a mental note for it not to happen again. Remember Chapter 2 about leaving the past behind? 'People say, "I'm going to be rejected because my mum rejected me and my boyfriend rejected me,"' explains life strategist Pete Cohen. 'So what? The only meaning that rejection has is the meaning that you give it. Life is full of difficulties, but that's when learning opportunities are staring you in the face. When things go wrong, it's the people who want to learn about life that can move on. No one said life is easy and no one said dating is easy. But if you have the right attitude of "I'm going to enjoy my life" and keep that picture out there of what I want to happen, then who knows what can happen?'

MOVING FORWARD

In some ways, the second date that you have with someone is even more enlightening than the first. On a first date both parties are often so wrapped up with their nerves that if there is chemistry between the two of you and there are sparks flying from the outset, the rest of the date can be a bit of blur. You both go into 'first date mode' of answering each other's questions and going through the motions of being ideal date material, rather than relaxing into who you are. The second time you meet, the other person will have had time to think about specific questions they may want to ask you, study you more closely and the date will be that much more 'serious' simply because you have committed to date number two.

Date number two can be really exciting, but remember to keep taking it slowly.

Just because you have made some kind of statement to say, 'I liked you so much the first time around I'm ready to commit to the second', you're not quite at the stage to plan the wedding yet! Keep things light and just enjoy yourself. Even if you are fuelled with lust and could quite happily declare undying love for the person, remember to take it slowly. You don't want to scare the other person – or indeed yourself – away by making radical statements too early into the relationship. As you move forward and the second date becomes a third, a fourth and then a proper relationship scenario, in order to give it the best possible chance of success you should get to grips with the golden rules of relationships:

PACE YOURSELF

Give yourself time – time to get to know each other, time for yourself, time to make the right decisions and time to communicate. It doesn't matter at what stage you are in a relationship, every couple should plan time to catch up with each other to assess how the relationship is going. It's a way of keeping track of your relationship and can help you avoid flare-ups and get to grips with situations that might be unclear. 'Put time aside to talk to each other properly,' says Relate counsellor Denise Knowles. 'That way if something has pissed you off you have the time to think about why they might have done it and how you feel about it. By giving each other time out from a situation you may realise that he/she was right in the first place and so you will have avoided confrontation.'

No matter how close the two of you are in a relationship, don't try and second guess how the other person feels about any situation. People make huge assumptions about how people should be treated based on how they would like to be treated themselves. For example, if someone looks as if they have a problem, it might feel like a natural reaction for you to say, 'Come on, let's talk about this,' whereas other people might say, 'Leave him/her alone, they need their own space.' Denise says that the best compromise is to make the offer that you are ready and willing to help, but not feel rejected if your offer is turned down. 'Say, "Is there something that I can help you with or would you prefer some time on your own?" That way you will have covered both sides of the situation. You are there for them, but you respect that they need their own space.'

Similarly, at some stage you may feel ready to move the relationship forward. But just because you feel it's time to do the parent thing, go out to dinner with his/her mates and do all of the 'couply' things that people in a relationship are 'supposed' to do, just put the brakes on a little. Consider how your other half may feel about those relationship milestones. 'Meeting the parents is definitely something that has to be negotiated and gauged on an individual basis,' says Denise. Do it too soon and you can send out all of the wrong signals. Getting to grips with one new person is difficult enough without having to cope with the whole of their family and friends too. In our 'fast forward' world, we forget how important key stages are in relationships and meeting the parents is certainly one of them – even though both parties may protest otherwise.

Friends often put the pressure on to meet the new person in your life, but again, you need to take things slowly. Just because you love your best mates to death doesn't mean to say that your new man/woman will have the same instant affection for them. The opposite may be true, in fact. They may take one look at them and think, 'Oh no, if this is her best friend then she is going to be around an awful lot...'

On the other side of the coin, make sure that you don't feel rushed into meeting your new squeeze's parents/friends/family. Even if you are both very casual about the encounters they are all loaded situations that subliminally can say a lot more than you may want to admit, both to yourself and to each other. Keep reminding yourself and your boyfriend/girlfriend that there's no rush to form a relationship. If your body clock is constantly reminding you that you're running out of child-bearing years, put a muffler on it for a while and just enjoy getting to know each other at your own pace. A month of clear thinking won't make any difference in the grand scheme of things.

MAKE IT SPECIAL

The first few weeks of any relationship can be amazing, but when the honeymoon period is over it's often back to normality with a bang (and a whimper). It's virtually impossible to sustain a relationship at the same level as the first flush of love, not to mention exhausting, so once a relationship settles into a pattern it's important to keep the spark alive. 'Keep doing special things,' says Denise. 'They don't have to be great big grand gestures, you could just send a sexy text message, put a note on the car window or plan some impromptu tickets to somewhere you know he/she would like to go.' People too often forget that you have to keep working on a relationship for it to be a success. Of course, you have to be able to relax into it but the more you put into the romance, the more you're likely to get back.

KEEP TALKING

Think about what you were like ten years ago. The chances are you had very different ideas than you do now and may feel like a different person all together. Your opinions about life have changed and you probably feel more 'grown up' than you used to. What people forget is that we all carry on changing and it's important to be able to grow with someone. 'Again and again I see couples whose relationship has broken down because they don't talk any more,' Denise says. It may sound like a bit of a cliché, or a Cliff Richard song, but how many couples have you seen in restaurants that sit there not saying a word to each other? 'I recently saw a couple and the husband said that he had given up talking to his wife because she always snapped at him,' says Denise. 'Meanwhile, she said that he had stopped talking to her and only showed her affection when he wanted sex. We established that they both desperately wanted to talk to each other and that somewhere along the line they had just stopped talking.' Remind yourself that we do change and, like second-guessing people, don't assume that people will always react the same way that they have always done about a situation. 'Once this particular couple realised that they had both matured in certain respects and that the woman would no longer get stressed over the same things that she used to, they could move forward in their relationship.'

BE YOURSELF

Everyone has expectations about their relationships but everyone is an individual and you have to keep reminding yourself of the fact. Our idiosyncrasies are what makes us unique and that's why we fall in love with each other in the first place. So there's really no point in ever trying to change anyone or trying to be anyone other than yourself. You can try, but it's unsustainable and really, wouldn't you rather that someone just loves you for who you are?

AND FINALLY...

At the end of the day, having a relationship with someone shouldn't be the major consideration of your life. As if you need any reminding, life's not a rehearsal and we only get one crack at it. What is the point of mooning around feeling sorry for yourself because you are single? You are hardly going to get people breaking your door down to be with you, are you?

The best news is that being single doesn't mean that you're on the shelf, it just means that you still have lots of living and maybe loving to do. You are in the perfect position to steer your life in a different direction, but you have to do something to make it happen. In the same way that if you are overweight you have to look at your food intake and how much exercise you are doing, if you are single (and don't want to be) you have to analyse your lifestyle and take a good look at yourself from the inside out.

Because there is a whole network of dating opportunities and literally thousands of people who are just like you and of a similar age, the only person stopping you doing anything about it is you. Do yourself a favour – make some phone calls, put some feelers out about what's going on in the area that you live in, then call a single friend and tell her/him that you've got a plan...

CASE STUDY

Poppy had a very tempestuous start to her relationship with Sean, but twenty years on they are still together and very much in love.

I was working with a girl called Amanda who was still sharing a flat with her ex-boyfriend, Sean. One night I had to call her house to pass on a message to him that she was going to be late and I just fell in love with Sean's voice. It was the most bizarre emotional feeling and the following Monday I said, 'Wow, Amanda, his voice is amazing,' and she said, 'Funny you should say that because he said the same about you!' That night he came to pick up Amanda from work and he was just drop-dead gorgeous.

Anyway, about a week later it was Amanda's birthday and I went over to help her prepare the food and Sean rolled in drunk about 9 p.m. We were introduced and I soon realised that we had absolutely nothing in common and I found him really difficult to talk to. But as the wine kicked in we became more relaxed and we were still talking when everyone had gone home. Amanda had said that I could stay over in the spare room which turned out to have a dirty old sleeping bag in it and no pillows or anything else. It was a freezing cold night (5 November 1982 to be precise) so when Sean suggested I stayed with him I thought, 'Great! At least I'll be warmer.' Well, one thing lead to another and we ended up having a wonderful night together. The next morning I woke up in love with him, pure and simple, it was like, 'Ping!' but I really thought it was just a one-night stand and I'd probably never see him again.

The next night I just couldn't cope with not seeing him so I begged my flatmate to drive us to north London (we lived in south London at the time) and I called Amanda's number knowing she wouldn't be there. Sean answered and I made up some spurious excuse about calling and then casually said, 'Oh, we're going to be in the Tufnell Park Tavern if you fancy coming along for a drink,' which amazingly he did. The next day I couldn't stop thinking about him and I called everyone at work Sean – even Amanda. Then it became too obvious and I told Amanda what had happened and she said she thought he was a filthy cradle snatcher! I was 22 and he was 31.

Anyway, a couple of weeks passed and I hadn't heard from him and really thought nothing was ever going to happen when he called me and asked me out to dinner. We had a lovely dinner and got completely smashed then he came back to my place and we started seeing each other from that moment on. At that stage we were just seeing each other at the weekends and monogamy didn't really ring true with him so to start off with it was really pretty hard. He told me that he loved me on the New Year's Eve after we had met, then said he'd changed his mind a few months later and didn't really know what he felt, so it was all very up and down to begin with. We moved in together, split up, got back together again and it was really tempestuous and we had filthy rows. Technically I had my own flat but I hardly ever stayed there, but one night when I was out with the girls I suddenly got the feeling that Sean was with someone else. I went to the flat and sure enough he was there with another woman. As she scrabbled to get her clothes on and head out of the flat I said, 'Where the hell do you think you're going?' and made Sean give her a lift home. I had nothing against her, I was just furious with Sean.

The next weekend he took me to Paris to try and make amends and we had the most wonderfully romantic weekend together but I was consumed with jealousy and continued to be obsessed with it for the next year. If I didn't know his movements from one moment to the next it would tear me up inside. Eventually Sean couldn't cope with it any more and split up with me and I was totally devastated.

After about three months I realised I just had to move on and get on with my life, then I got a call from Sean in the middle of the night totally out of the blue. He asked if he could come over and I said yes, but I refused to turn any lights on and we talked in the dark for hours. Finally he asked me to sit next to him and you could almost see the crackle of electricity between us, then one thing lead to another and we spent the rest of the night together.

Overnight I decided that if we were going to get back together it had to be on very different terms. I thought that he would think he could walk in and out of my life whenever he wanted, so I was very low key about it all and told him that he shouldn't assume we were back together just because we'd slept with each other. After that we started seeing each other very slowly. The rules had changed as far as I was concerned and we eventually moved in together and bought a flat.

A couple of years later I gave him an ultimatum that I really wanted to get married and have children. Sean had always said he wouldn't get married and I respected his ideals but I told him that I'd made up my mind and if he didn't want to be with me then we should split up. A few months later he proposed to me and we got married on 30 June 1989. We'd been married for just over a year when our son Tom was born but although we tried for more children and had IVF it wasn't meant to be.

On 5 November 2002 it was twenty years since we met and because we'd had so much upheaval in the first few years it meant we'd got over all our relationship difficulties in the beginning. We still have the occasional stinking row and I'll sleep in the spare room but I think we're very mutually supportive. I've learned that if you stand back and wait and be focused in what you want in life that things can work out. Sean says he loves me every single day and we always set the alarm fifteen minutes early in the morning so that we can have a hug. It somehow balances the day – whatever else we have to face we know we have support.

Of course we've both changed enormously over the years – we're twenty years older for a kick off and have all the life experience to go with it. I think to make any relationship work you need support, trust (which in our case took a long time to rebuild) and these come out of loving someone in the right way.

CASE STUDY

Finally, if you needed any more convincing that giving yourself a little bit of extra help is a good idea in the dating game, read Andrea and Jonathon's story.

Andrea: *In 1991 I decided to put an ad in London's weekly listings' magazine, Time Out. At the time I worked for a women's magazine and so it was a very female industry and I was fed up with just going out with people from the media. I thought there had to be someone else out there and I knew I had to do something different to break out of the cycle I was in. I also thought that putting an ad in would be a laugh and a bit of an ego boost because I'd get to meet lots of people. I'd been talking to my best friend about doing it and one day I thought, what the hell, just do it! I sat down and it probably took me about two hours to compose the ad and the wording was:*

WARM WITTY FEMINIST, 27, SEEKS RIGHT ON DUDE *(which sounds terrible now, at the time it sounded fine!)* LIKES ARTS, FUN AND PEANUT BUTTER. ONLY KIND CARING SOULS NEED APPLY, THE REST OF YOU SHOULD BE ASHAMED OF YOURSELVES

It cost about £35 to place the ad and I was really in debt at the time but I had to do it before I changed my mind! I sent it all off and about two weeks later my first batch of letters arrived in a big brown envelope. I remember opening it up and thinking, 'Oh my God!' There were about forty letters and I immediately rang my friend and told her what I'd done and she came over. Then we went through them together automatically putting them in 'yes', 'no' and 'maybe' piles. I'd say about 80 per cent of people had sent photos even though I deliberately didn't request them. I thought if I'm going to go out there and do something different it's important for me to break out of what I think is my type and just be really open and see what happens. I wrote back to everyone who wrote to me and I ended up getting about eighty letters, so I spent another fortune sending replies to all of them!

In total I met eight people from the ad. I have to say that the thing that attracted me first were their pictures and then if their letters were good too I was even more interested. I did meet people who didn't send photos but who sounded interesting and funny.

When I wrote back to them I told them a little bit about what I looked like and said I had long curly red hair because people tend either really to like it or hate it. I didn't want to identify myself too much about what I did, I just did a nice chatty letter to them because I thought if they'd put the effort in I'd do the same. Some people just wrote two lines and some people even sent photocopied letters! And in those cases I thought if you can't even be bothered to write a letter, forget it. What I did with the ones I was interested in was write to them and give them my number so they had the opportunity to decide if they wanted to meet me.

I'd always meet people for a drink first and depending on how we got on and how early or late it was we'd go for a meal. I ended up going for meals with most of them because I felt awkward about saying no and I also felt that I needed to be open about giving each date a real try. I ended up spending about three hours with most people unless it was really obvious that it just wasn't going to happen. One guy sent me a letter and it was really funny and we met up and he produced a rose out of his breast pocket while we were having dinner! Part of me thought, 'Oh, that's so sweet!' and part of me thought, 'Get me out of here!' I just thought it was really *inappropriate – I'd known him two hours and red roses are so symbolic. So we had the meal and I tried to be nice without being overly friendly and I think he got the message. I left the rose which is probably mean and the wrong thing to do but the whole thing was too weird.*

Meanwhile. . .

Jonathon: *I'd moved down to Stevenage from the north in 1989 and most of my friends lived in London. I'd just broken up my with my girlfriend and was pretty sure I wasn't going to meet anyone where I lived and I couldn't have a relationship with anyone at work because I'm in personnel. I used to read Time Out every week because I spent so much time in London and when I split up with my girlfriend I thought I'd do something that I didn't normally do and have a look at the personals ads. I loved Andrea's ad and it made me laugh – especially the bit that said 'the rest of you should be ashamed of yourselves'. I decided to reply to her ad and wrote a really silly letter with really bad drawings on it and stuck it in the mail. Oh, I also stuck a photo in with the letter. She hadn't asked for one but I thought I should send one anyway but the only one I had was a picture of me at Loch Lomond with my eyes shut!*

Andrea: *The fact he had his eyes shut really made me laugh! A lot of people had obviously chosen their pictures really carefully and some were a little bit posed but here was someone who didn't have a huge ego and I thought that was quite sweet. So I sent him a long chatty letter back and did lots of silly drawings too.*

Jonathon: *I was surprised to get Andrea's letter because I thought she'd be more likely to ring me. Anyway, I decided to call her and we planned to meet upstairs in a pub in Soho.*

Andrea: *It was quarter to eight on a Wednesday night and I was a little bit late. Jonathon said he'd be wearing a leather jacket and holding a copy of Time Out and I recognised him straight away – even though he had his eyes open!*

Jonathon: *I was really nervous but I liked Andrea straight away because she's very easy to talk to but we were both in professional mode because she's a journalist and I interview people for a living so we just interviewed each other!*

Andrea: *I knew what Jonathon looked like so I knew that I was attracted to him and the more I got talking to him, the more I liked him. The one thing that I was concerned about was that he seemed really quiet and that worried me because in past relationships I was always the one who said let's do this and let's do that and I didn't want to be in that situation again. Anyway, two days later he rang me and said he'd bought tickets for a band I really liked and I was so bowled over that he'd taken the initiative that I was really impressed.*

Jonathon: *Our second date was a bit tense because after the first date I knew I liked her and wanted to see her again. We went to St James's Park and sat on a bench and had a really good chat and were both really relaxed. We went to the cinema and had a snog afterwards!*

Andrea: *I was talking to him on the escalator and he suddenly gave me this huge snog! And he had this big smile on his face! The only trouble was that I was seeing other people at the time and I told him about this other guy called Steve who I'd arranged to meet for a second date and Jonathon was a bit pissed off about it. I thought it was better to be totally straight with him, but he got quite upset and then I got upset too!*

Jonathon: *I was upset because it just made me doubt a lot of things and I wondered if she was just a fake. I thought we had a good thing going, so why would she even want to see anyone else? I decided that I should just call it off if she decided she wanted to see other people as well as me.*

Andrea: *When I met Steven again I just thought he was a bit of a prat and I immediately regretted what I'd said to Jonathon. I spent the whole evening thinking about Jonathon and when I got in I called him immediately. I said I was really really sorry and wanted to make up for it and he sounded really lovely and we arranged to meet up again.*

Jonathon: *I felt a whole lot better after Andrea had called and we met up again and had a really lovely date, then arranged to see each other the following weekend.*

Andrea: *I told him to bring his toothbrush! It was all so lovely. We went out for a really romantic meal, then saw Jules et Jim which* was really romantic and then he came back to mine. It just felt totally right and after that we just went on from there.

Jonathon: *I'd been saving up to buy a flat and about six months later I moved to London and Andrea came to stay with me quite a lot. She was determined to keep her independence and kept her flat for a while but soon realised that to all intents and purposes she was living with me and she eventually moved in properly.*

Andrea: *I was in denial for six months! I had this idea in my head that when you are a couple it really changes you as an individual and you stop doing things you want to do and lose your independence. I didn't want to become one of those people that gets so immersed in their relationship that you stop being your own person. We never had a big sit-down discussion about whether I'd move in, it just felt like a really natural progression. I remember telling people that we'd moved in and them saying, 'Oh, you'll be getting married soon,' and it was like 'argh!' I was really anti-marriage at the time and didn't see the point of it as we didn't have to prove our commitment to each other. I was also scared that if we were married we'd start taking each other for granted and I didn't want to take on the stereotypical roles that my own parents had in their relationship. I don't know why, but I thought getting married would suddenly turn us into these people. We kept saying we were going to have a 'not getting married' party, but then we started talking about the possibility of children in a vague way and things started to change.*

Jonathon: *We both said that if we ever did have children we'd prefer to be married and then we started talking about what marriage would actually mean for us. Then once we started talking about what the day itself could be like we started to get really excited!*

Andrea: *We got married on 5 July 1997 – six years and three days after we'd met and we had the best time ever. When we were planning our wedding we both wrote down what the three most important things about our wedding should be.*

We ended up changing the vows a little (the word obey wasn't in there!) and we had a truly wonderful day and went to Australia and New Zealand for our honeymoon.

Jonathon:*To start off with we didn't tell people how we met. I was quite open about it but Andrea is more private and at the beginning she thought she would be judged by it because there's still such a stigma involved.*

Andrea:*I thought it sounded a bit desperate that we'd met through lonely hearts and I was a bit worried about what people would think. There is such a stigma attached to it which is a real shame. I hope that things will change though and people will become more accepting of dating agencies, lonely hearts and things like that. I strongly believe that if you're not meeting the right people and you're disappointed with what's happening in your relationships then why keep doing the same thing if it's not working? You have to break out of old habits and do something different. And you've also got to do it with a certain sense of humour. Neither Jonathon nor I did this thinking that we'd meet the person we were going to spend the rest of our lives with. But doing something like this means you are meeting people who are emotionally available, actually available, that are interested in what you are interested in. So it kind of whittles everything down. Some people don't think it's exactly romantic but there's this myth that you are going to bump into someone in a book shop or walking your dog but that only happens in films! As a woman, doing something like this means you are completely in the driving seat, you can choose who you want to meet and the ball is in your court.*

And it might even end in happy ever after. . .

DATING DATA – POINTS TO REMEMBER

→ Use dating experiences positively and have a laugh about the ones that didn't go quite so well. Don't beat yourself up about disasters.
→ If you're not interested in someone, don't string them along.
→ If you like someone but there wasn't any chemisty between the two of you, think of swapping numbers or keeping in touch anyway for future dates or possibilities for your single friends.
→ If he/she doesn't call, he/she isn't interested. Period.
→ Keep taking things slowly. Just because you may be on date number two, three or four, it doesn't mean that a wedding is on the cards.
→ Give yourself lots of time to make considered decisions about your relationships.

→ Don't try and second guess someone or presume that they will react to situations in the same way as you.

→ Don't let your friends pressurize you into moving the relationship forward too quickly.

→ Keep the relationship special, especially when the 'honeymoon' period is well and truly over.

→ Keep talking to each other and keep working on your friendship.

→ If all else fails, celebrate the fact that you are single and that you still have so many possibilites in front of you.

RESOURCES

The Association of British Dating Agencies (ABIA)
35 Market Street
Tamworth
Staffordshire
B19 7LR
0845 345 2242
www.abia.org.uk
email: enquiries@abia.org.uk
The governing body of British dating agencies with around 35 members who follow a stringent code of practice supported by the Office of Fair Trading. Via the ABIA, consumers have access to safeguard procedures including (if necessary) independent arbitration. The ABIA's code of practice is outlined on their website (see above) which also has Dos and Don'ts of Dating, a full list of members and links to other useful sites.

* ABIA members

PERSONAL INTRODUCTION AGENCIES
The most expensive, but generally considered to be the most effective kind of dating agency. Personal introduction agencies interview potential members before they are accepted on to their books and then hand pick suitable matches. Each agency varies slightly and offers different membership packages.

Club Sirius
0870 745 1745
www.clubsirius.co.uk
Offers a 'matching service for considerate, articulate people where they are in full control of their own lifestyle choices.' Members receive personal introductions, singles' holiday details, social events calendar and a full-colour magazine, giving descriptions of all their members.

Drawing Down the Moon*
(Head Office)
Adam & Eve Mews
165–169 Kensington High Street
London
W8 6SH
020 7937 6263
www.drawingdownthemoon.co.uk
The UK's oldest introduction service that specialises in matching
'thinking people' who are generally educated to degree level or
higher. Potential new members are interviewed and then matched
by the team of Drawing Down the Moon matchmakers. Drawing
Down the Moon is also connected to Only Lunch and the internet
dating site www.loveandfriends.com.

Sarah Eden Introductions*
(Head Office)
Eden House
38 Thames Street
Windsor
Berkshire
SL4 1PR
01753 830 350
London office 020 7499 9626
www.sara-eden.co.uk
One of the more expensive introduction agencies but boasting an
excellent success rate, Sarah Eden offers different tiers of
membership to 'attractive, compatible, eligible single people'
including an Executive membership for its 'high profile' members.
Extra club activities include cocktail parties and trips to Ascot,
Henley Regatta and Wimbledon.

Elite Introductions
0870 780 1510
www.eliteintroductions.com
As its website confirms, Elite is not a dating agency. 'All our
members are seriously looking for a committed relationship,' it
says. Representatives interview potential members in their homes
to get a more detailed insight into their lifestyle and then hand pick
potential dates. Linked with Club Sirius.

Gorgeous Networks
020 7731 0033
www.gg-t.com
Gorgeous Networks say it is an 'unashamedly elitist speed dating and
networking agency for gorgeous people'. As well as matchmaking,
founder Lorraine Adams also offers date coaching classes (see below).

Only Lunch*
Adam & Eve Mews
165–169 Kensington High Street
London
W8 6SH
www.onlylunch.co.uk
0800 908900
Owned by Drawing Down the Moon (see above), the Only Lunch
matchmakers interview new members and a team of matchmakers
select and set up lunch dates (or early suppers) on a 'blind date'
basis. 'There's no pressure – it's Only Lunch.'

LIST AGENCIES
These agencies operate mainly by post, therefore no one-to-one
selection interviews are carried out. Matches are made either by
computer (as with Dateline) or by human cupids and then a list of
potential dates is sent to the member. Depending on the agency,
contact details are either sent immediately or after profiles have
been shortlisted by the member.

Caroline Crowther*
The Old Coach House
Wedmore
Somerset
BS28 4BZ
01934 712900
www.carolinecrowther.com
An agency for the 28–65+ age group which caters for people in the
south, west and southwest of England and south Wales. Members
are offered five personally matched introduction plans. They are
sent profiles of potential dates and then telephone numbers are
exchanged.

Dateline
0800 0343345
www.dateline.co.uk
The UK's leading 'list' introduction service. No face-to-face
interviews; membership is handled by telephone, post and the
internet. Members fill in a detailed questionnaire (including
categories such as religion, political stance and attitudes) and a
computer matches you with at least three other members
according to where you live and the type of person who you would
like to meet. You then receive a list of matches and their contact
details within a few days. You are also invited to advertise in the
Dateline newsletter and record an advertisement for the Dateline
Connections service.

Initial Approach*
4 Beech Road
Dunblane
FK15 0LA
Scotland
01786 825777
www.initial-approach.co.uk
Scotland's premier introduction and social events agency with over
1,000 members

Just Woodland Friends*
Stable Lodge
Pant Glas Farm
Sennybridge
Brecon
LD3 8SS
01874 636909
www.justwoodlandfriends.com
An introduction service aimed at 20–50 year olds who are involved
with farming, wildlife, equestrianism, country sports, dog training
and so on, 'Members who really understand what country life is all
about and who want to meet new friends of the opposite sex with
the possibility of forming a relationship.' The website also gives
details of Irish Woodland Friends and Autumn Friends for those
aged 40–75.

Kids No Object
01243 543685
www.kno.org.uk
Designed for single parents and childless single people, KNO also
runs Partners for Parents in the Greater London area. It costs £70
for life membership. All male applicants are vetted against the
Sexual Offenders Register.

Singles Grapevine*
Station House
Blunham
Bedfordshire
01767 641259
www.singlesgrapevine.com
With its unique 'opt-in' membership, Singles Grapevine updates its
members list every three months to ensure all members are
actively looking for dates. In other words, you won't sign up and be
matched up with someone who's no longer available. Standard
membership provides 18–24 matches within a 30-mile radius of
your home. Different membership tiers are offered including free
trials.

Vegetarian Matchmakers*
Concord House
7 Waterbridge Court
Appleton
Warrington
Cheshire
WA4 3BJ
01925 601609
www.veggiematchmakers.com
Established in 1980, VMM is a dating agency for vegetarians and
vegans. It also offers 'friendship, social events, opportunities for
members to publicise their own businesses and a commitment to
develop other services of interest to the vegetarian and vegan
community.' Members often have certain interests in common such
as animal welfare and the environment.

ACTIVITY AGENCIES

A slightly more subtle way of meeting fellow single people, activity agencies create opportunities for people to meet socially and a strong emphasis is put on meeting new friends, not just matchmaking.

40datesAnight
020 8458 4069
www.40datesAnight.co.uk
Speed-dating to the max! At a 40 Dates a Night event, 40 single men and 40 single women meet in a bar/club/hotel for cocktails and canapes. Each man and woman get three minutes to chat and then move on to the next 'date.' At the end of the night, everyone completes a form evaluating each person they have met with a tick for a 'Yes, I fancy them' or an F for 'Just friends'. Then the 40 Dates a Night matchmakers forward email addresses to whoever is mutually attracted. The rest is up to you!

The AL Arts Club
020 7722 2878
www.artisticlicense.co.uk
A north London arts social club for 30–50 year olds. Members meet once a month at the club HQ art gallery for drinks, exhibitions, concerts, theatre trips and other arts events.

Across the Room
0800 591274
www.acrosstheroom.co.uk
Weekly events for single people in their thirties, forties and fifties in the Essex, Hertfordshire, Kent and Suffolk area. It costs £125 for lifetime membership, plus the price of each event (from £15–40).

Culture Lovers
0800 096 9950
www.culturelovers.com
Whether you want to make new friends (of either sex), meet new companions to go to concerts, the theatre, cinema and other cultural events, or find romance, culturelovers brings together (mostly) thirty- and forty-somethings from London and the home

counties. Events are twice or three times a month and around
12–30 of the clubs 250-strong membership attend each. It costs
£180 for a year's membership.

Club Six
0870 606 4646
www.clubsix.com
Monthly dinner dates for busy professionals. As the name
suggests, each party consists of six people (three men, three
women) dining at a broad range of top London restaurants, 'to
extend their business and social network – or perhaps something
more . . .' Membership costs from £45 for a one-off event to £215
for premium annual membership.

Dinner Dates
08704 424243
www.dinnerdates.com
The UK's original social events agency with 14,000 members,
offering a calendar of social events including black tie and other
dinner parties, buffets, balls, cocktail parties and various other
outdoor and cultural events. Membership, £150 (plus VAT), plus the
cost of each event.

Eligible Balls
connect@theinsight.co.uk
Monthly singles parties for 25-year-olds upwards held in Brighton
where guests are encouraged to play 'low key' matching games.
£20 a ticket including a free drink.

Intervarsity Club
London office
203 Bedford Chambers
The Piazza
Covent Garden
London
WC2E 8HA
020 7240 0487
www.ivc.org.uk
The UK's original multi-activity club which was set up as a place

for graduates to meet and mix. The IVC offers activities-orientated weekends all over the UK (walking, watersports, biking and so on), plus fitness, cultural and social events around the UK. The various local Intervarsity clubs around the UK have a combined total of 1,300 members between the ages of 25-45 (although there are no age limits for who can join).

The Renaissance Club
0870 737 2582
www.rclub.co.uk
Private members club run via the internet with around 3,000 members. Membership costs £145 and includes a package of discounts and deals including free drinks at top bars, memberships at clubs, discounts at leading restaurants and invitations for key events and private parties.

REGULAR COURSES ON FLIRTING, DATING AND CONFIDENCE
Pete Cohen
www.petecohen.com
email info@tvpete.com
Best known for his appearances on *GMTV's Inch Loss Island*, Pete Cohen is a personal trainer and life coach specialising in weight loss, phobias and confidence building. He offers one-to-one counselling and habit-busting courses.

The Flirting Academy – Peta Heskell
0700 435 4784
www.flirtzone.com
Quarterly flirting workshops (sorry, playshops) in central London for late twenties upwards. Prices from £220 (depending on time of booking). Each course covers a range of flirting techniques and information including humour, seduction, dancing, movement, using personal space, sexuality, body language, dealing with rejection and the power of compliments.

Singles Seminars
Contact Mary Balfour
C/o Drawing Down the Moon
020 7937 6263

Semi-regular seminars on dating dos and don'ts including confidence building, body language, grooming and dating behaviour

Date Coaching
Gorgeous Networks
020 7731 0033
www.gg-t.com
Date coach Lorraine Adams will tell you 'what your best friend won't' about your dating techniques – or lack of them! £45 for an hour's date coaching consultation. You are then set up on two dummy dates with your performance rated (or slated) after each one.

INTERNET DATING SITES
Most internet dating sites work on the same principle – you log on, state whether you are a man or a woman looking to meet a man or a woman and the age range that you prefer. You are then shown (mostly for free) a number of matches and generally it's at this stage that you have to commit to some kind of membership, although there are online dating agencies which offer a week's free trial. The sites also vary on how much information is needed for each profile – from very basic one-line descriptions (www.twoscompany.co.uk) to extremely detailed personality breakdowns (www.loveandfriends.com).

www.datingdeluxe.com
Submit your details for free and browse suitable matches from all around the world. You can choose what kind of relationship you want, ranging from 'hang out' to 'long term'

www.loveandfriends.com
This site is geared towards people educated to university level (or above), with probably the most detailed personality data question and personal requirement sheet.

www.oneandonly.com
Choose whether to select ads by geographical location, age, physical characteristics, lifestyle or photos. The 'Agent of Love' service scans new ads daily and emails you details that match up with your preferences.

www.onesaturday.com
Create a free profile and browse other members for free.

www.pearmatch.co.uk
'The world is your orchard' says Pearmatch, who offer a special 'ice breaker' service: your profile is supplied to your matches at the same time that you receive theirs, so that you both know something about each other before you get in touch.

www.twoscompany.co.uk
No photos of members, just text information with telephone number contact boxes. It's free to place an ad but costs 60p per minute to listen to calls. Also includes text messaging and a WAP service.

www.wejustclicked.com
One of the better designed sites with different scales and choices of membership including Gold membership which has access to chat rooms and Pink for the gay community. SMS messaging, sexy surveys and success stories are also featured.

www.wheresmydate.com
Fun and funky website that offers a week's free membership and the chance to view and submit more quirky personality details – what they call 'can openers'. For example 'Rollercoasters – scary or cool?' and 'What age were you when you discovered Father Christmas didn't exist?'

HOLIDAY COMPANIES THAT OFFER SINGLES' HOLIDAYS
Solo's Holidays
08700 720 700
www.solosholidays.co.uk
Holidays, breaks and events designed exclusively for unattached, divorced, widowed or separated people and offered in specific age ranges (25–45, 28–55 and 45–69). Each group is accompanied by a tour manager and rooms are on a single occupancy basis. Over 800 holidays per year to over 70 countries.

SINGLES' HOLIDAYS COMPANIES ON THE WEB
www.encounter.co.uk
From simple cultural explorations to really wild adventures for
groups of 6–21 for 20s and 30s, including the Sahara, Timbuktu,
the Inca Trail and the Amazon. On an Encounter tour you are not a
passenger but part of the club team and expected to join in the
club activities such as cooking and camp chores.

www.solitairhols.co.uk
Holiday solutions for single travellers and small groups including
short breaks and party weekends. Solitair prides itself on
attracting and mixing a cross section of age groups from mid-20s
to 60s from all around the world.

www.travel-quest.co.uk
Singles holidays, short break getaways, singles weekends and solo
vacations from around thirty companies offering singles packages
including yoga and walking in France, wine tours and Edinburgh art
breaks.

www.trekamerica.com
32 camping adventure tours from seven days to nine weeks in the
USA for 18–38-year-olds. Also incorporating Footloose holidays for
older travellers.

FURTHER READING

Bushnell, Candace, *Sex and the City*, Abacus, 1999

Cohen, Pete, *Fear Busting*, HarperCollins, 2003

Cohen, Pete with Cummings, Sten, *Habit Busting*, HarperCollins, 2000

Cox, Tracey, *Supersex*, Dorling Kindersley, 2002

Darwin, Charles, edited by Ekman, Paul, *The Expression of the Emotions in Man and Animals*, Fontana Press, 1999

Fein, Ellen & Schneider, Sherrie, *The Rules*, HarperCollins, 1995

Fielding, Helen, *Bridget Jones's Diary*, Picador, 1997

Heskell, Peta, *Flirt Coach*, Thorson's, 2001

Heskell, Peta, *The Little Book of Flirting*, Thorson's, 2002

Jeffers, Susan, *Feel the Fear and Do It Anyway*, Rider, 1997

Pease, Allan, *Body Language*, Sheldon Press, 1997

Reeves, Richard, *Happy Mondays: Putting the Pleasure Back Into Work*, Momentum, 2001

Schwartz, Pepper, *Everything You Know About Love and Sex Is Wrong: Twenty-Five Relationship Myths Redefined to Achieve Happiness and Fulfillment in Your Intimate Life*, Perigee, 2001

ACKNOWLEDGEMENTS

The biggest thank you ever goes to my great friend Anita Naik who suggested that I should write this book and has been an incredible inspiration and source of information. Also to the many dating experts that agreed to be interviewed for the book including Pete Cohen, Denise Knowles, Karen Mooney and Mary Balfour. Although I have changed most of the names in the case studies, it still took some convincing to get people to talk about their love life (or lack of it) so a big thank you to all of you.

INDEX

Buying a Home: The Virgin Guide
Ben West

Buying a home is likely to be the biggest financial transaction of your life and can be a source of great stress if you get it wrong. Even when things go right there are many potential problems. This book steers you through the property maze comprehensively to help you find exactly the home you want. It's packed with information on all aspects of housing, including renting, buying, leasehold, selling, estate agents, making offers, dealing with solicitors, mortgages and surveys.

0 7535 0773 0
£7.99

Entertaining: The Virgin Guide
Eleni Kyriacou

you're an aspiring Nigella Lawson or Jamie Oliver, *Entertaining: The Virgin Guide* will help you on your way! The book is the complete guide to entertaining, whether you want to host an formal dinner for friends or a full-scale blow-out in a hired hall. Full of down-to-earth advice from experts in the field, it is ideal for busy people who want to enjoy themselves at their own parties and create the kind of events that will be remembered for all the right reasons.

0 7535 0749 8
£7.99

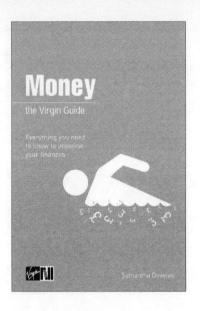

Money: The Virgin Guide
Samantha Downes

Most of us need a few pointers when it comes to financial issue
The author covers numerous useful topics in this jargon-free
guide: from the financial implications of moving in together o
getting married to controlling your credit and store card spendi
from mortgages and endowments to setting up companies.
Also included are a glossary of financial terms and a list of
useful addresses. This is a guide that you, quite literally,
can't afford to be without!

0 7535 0745 5
£7.99